Money Talks

MONEY TALKS

Language and Lucre
in American Fiction

Edited by Roy R. Male

Foreword by Ronald Schleifer

University of Oklahoma Press: Norman

Books by Roy R. Male

Hawthorne's Tragic Vision (Austin, 1957)
(coeditor) *American Literary Masters* (New York, 1965)
(editor) *Types of Short Fiction* (Belmont, California, 2d ed., 1970)
Enter, Mysterious Stranger (Norman, 1979)
(editor) *Money Talks: Language and Lucre in American Fiction* (Norman, 1981)

Copyright © 1980 by the University of Oklahoma for *Genre* magazine; assigned 1980 to the University of Oklahoma Press. New edition copyright © 1981 by the University of Oklahoma Press, Norman, Publishing Division of the University of Oklahoma. Manufactured in the U.S.A.

To Victor A. Elconin
teacher, leader, writer, and friend

CONTENTS

Foreword
  Ronald Schleifer — Page ix

Literature and Lucre: A Meditation
  Leslie A. Fiedler — 1

The Gold Bug
  Marc Shell — 11

The Image in the Mirror: The Double Economy of James's *Portrait*
  Edgar A. Dryden — 31

The Bought Generation: Another Look at Money in *The Sun Also Rises*
  Patrick D. Morrow — 51

Tales of Obscene Power: Money, Culture, and the Historical Fictions of E. L. Doctorow
  David S. Gross — 71

Contra Naturam?: Usury in William Gaddis's *JR*
  Steven Weisenburger — 93

The Soul's Husband: Money in *Humboldt's Gift*
  Steven T. Ryan — 111

Things I Left Out of My Autobiography or How Thorstein Veblen's Theory of Conspicuous Consumption Worked for Me
  Mark Harris — 123

Creatively Writing the Grippingly Erotic True Story
  Herbert Gold — 137

Index — 145

Foreword

Money talks, this book says. But how does it talk? Does it "talk dirty" as Herbert Gold suggests? Does it swear, as David Gross asserts? Does it mean what it says? Does it mean more than it says? David Gross begins his fine essay on the fiction of Doctorow with a personal confession of the "embarrassment of riches" that the subject of our book offers a Marxist, and throughout the essays collected here economic metaphors recur with surprising and delightful regularity. Thus Leslie Fiedler ends his meditation on language and lucre metaphorically crying all the way to the bank; Marc Shell begins his study of Poe's "Gold-Bug" with a section called "The Bug for Gold"; Edgar Dryden observes in his examination of *The Portrait of a Lady* that "the metaphors that James habitually uses to describe . . . art carry a heavy economic content," and he cites James's own observation that the reader tries to get "his experience as cheaply as possible"; Patrick Morrow opens his essay by saying that the treatment of money in Hemingway "is hardly a closed account"; Steven Weisenburger claims that "depreciation is the principal topic of Gaddis's *JR*"; and the last word of *Money Talks* is spoken by Herbert Gold himself. All these metaphors, like metal specie, are strangely literal; they indicate, in the context of our collection, the interest, the supplemental increase, that language, like money, can make. "Usury itself is the state of Nature," Weisenburger argues; ". . . even molecules exchange particles and give up energy (interest) during the transaction." The "interest" the language of commerce yields in these essays is the "interest" of puns: the interest of the literal significance strangely overlaid on the figurative phrase—what Mark Harris calls in his autobiographical piece the "verifying bonus" of money.

Money verifies because it is, for America, the great national myth: it stands in relation to America, Weisenburger suggests, in the same way that the Nibelung Ring stands in relation to Germany. Leslie Fiedler speaks of the novel as the great American form—as American as the commerce which gave the novel circulation, "invented even as we were inventing our Republic," invented in America to portray "Man's attempted mastery of Nature, . . . the frame [for which] is commerce"—and the relation of money to America is a submerged theme in the essays collected here. "If I'm obsessed with money," Steven Ryan quotes Bellow's Humboldt as saying, ". . . The reason is that we're Americans after all. What kind of American would I be if I were innocent about money . . . ? I go along with Horace Walpole. Walpole said it was natural for free men to think about money. Why? Because money *is* freedom, that's why." "America," Marc Shell notes, "was the historical birthplace of widespread paper money in the Western World," and with this historical fact a central concern of these essays—and a central concern of the novels they treat—is articulated: the relation between the symbolism of money and the value it represents or creates. Money, Fiedler says, is the "one universal currency"; and David Gross adds "money is important in fiction because it is at the source of the most important fictions in our lives."

Money, these essays suggest, is a fiction—it is perhaps the great American fiction—yet, like the puns I've mentioned, it takes on a literal significance which comes to dominate its fictional status. Punning, Shell asserts, makes something out of nothing so that paper money itself is a "pun": "in the institution of paper money, sign and substance, paper and gold, are clearly dissociated, much as word is dissociated from meaning in punning." Such paper creates the possibility of the usury that Aristotle decries:

> The most hated sort [of wealth-getting] . . . is usury, which makes a gain out of money itself, and not from the natural object of it. For money was intended to be used in exchange, but not to increase at interest. And this term interest, which means the birth of money from money, is applied to the breeding of money because the offspring resembles the parent. Wherefore of all modes of getting wealth this is the most unnatural.[1]

Thus, if interest is a "pun," money itself could be described by the figure James offers for the nature of fiction (which Dryden uses as the center of his examination of representation in James), the "image in the mirror": money, like the American government, is "representative." It is this quality of fiction, its ability to "represent" life as money "represents" value, that makes lucre such a useful figure for fiction, and makes the metaphor of money's speech, "money talks," so appropriate a focus for literary studies.

Thus I've returned to the questions with which I began: how does money talk? How is it related to the ways fiction "talks"? How is it, as Weisenburger claims and I have been suggesting, that there is an "apparent similarity (even identity) of money and language"? Money, Weisenburger goes on to say, "as a semiological system compares with the semiological systems of writing, painting, music"; "the distinction between substance and shadow in monetary and aesthetic theory," Shell says, "affects the understanding of symbolization in general and of linguistic representation in particular"; the "radical distrust of language," Gross argues, is intimately connected with the violence of "unnatural" money. Language and money are apparently similar—perhaps even identical—in that each is a medium to represent value that comes to be valuable in itself. (They are radically different as well: only a con-man can "buy" his lunch with words.) The literary work, Fiedler says most starkly, "remains incomplete until it has passed from the desk to the marketplace." That is, literature, like language in Saussure's examination of it, only has meaning in its currency, in its exchange: it is, as Aristotle said, "intended to be used in exchange." Yet that "exchange" can turn on itself to create, in another pun, its own "interest." At issue here is the question of value, the question of money as well as literature: "simple exchange value," Morrow quotes a character in *The Sun Also Rises* saying: "You give them money. They give you a stuffed dog." Money and fiction exchange values: for so much money you get this stuffed dog of a book. "Economic objects," Dryden says, "have meaning only in terms of exchange. . . . All other objects have a content from which they derive value, but money derives its content from its value—it represents the value of things without the things themselves." In this way there seems to be something essentially, "unnaturally," corrupt in money as Aristotle suggests.

Thus Steven Ryan says that much American fiction uses wealth "only to indicate disease," and Gross's reading of Doctorow and Weisenburger's reading of Gaddis seem to ratify his assertion. Money contaminates as "the economic metaphor contaminates the ideal of pure vision by way of notions of equivalence and exchange." In much the way Samuel Johnson derides the pun, that "usurious" form, and his contemporaries derided the corrupting power of fiction itself, money contaminates "things" by offering the means of seeing them, potentially or actually, in exchange, not solely themselves, embodying—in the strange "allegory" of commerce—what James calls a "very different story." "A quibble," Johnson wrote, "poor and barren as it is, gave [Shakespeare] such delight, that he was content to purchase it, by the sacrifice of reason, propriety and truth. A quibble was to him the fatal *Cleopatra* for which he lost the world, and was content to lose it."[2] That is the power and the problem of money: like fiction—like desire—it is always other than itself, incomplete as Fielder says, until it is exchanged.

Fiction is other than itself because it allows us, as James says, "to live at the expense of someone else." And at the heart of fiction, as at the heart of wealth, is the guilt of such a disproportionate exchange. It is the guilt of seeing truth in a lie, of utilizing power where there seems to be no responsibility, of sacrificing reason, propriety and truth to "purchase" delight. More than that, it is the guilt of suspecting that both the purchase and the price are illusory. "Truths are illusions," Nietzsche writes, "about which one has forgotten that this is what they are; metaphors which are worn out and without sensuous power; coins which have lost their pictures and now matter only as metal, no longer as coins."[3] Nietzsche is reversing, "exchanging," the metaphors with which I am dealing so that here coin is a figure for language rather than language—puns, fiction, figures of speech—being a figure for money and how it works, how it "talks." And this is just the point: since language and money exist only in exchange, they can, in fact, contaminate, purchase and lose truth, reason, and propriety, offer guilty delight.

The horror, of course, is that such delight comes to nothing. Nietzsche speaks of the metallic value remaining after the coin has lost its pictures, but this, Shell argues, is not operative in paper money, pictures without coin, which is, as Dryden says, "without content." "The guilty fear," Shell writes, "that all literature was, like money, in this sense, a merely passable 'naught,' a mere cipher, troubled Melville, an expert on confidence, for whom the tropic center of symbolization is an 'algebraic x' threatening language and money with devaluation and annihilation." This results in the constant threat of the "entropic" and "final Götterdammerung" Weisenburger sees in *JR*, the confusion of money and success that haunts Citrine in *Humboldt's Gift*, the guilt of the huckster that Fiedler describes, and the curious reservation the prostitute Herbert Gold meets displays, who knows how to do "dirty things" and hasn't just learned them for work, but won't "talk dirty for anyone." The horror and guilt of fiction, like that of money, is that it is a counterfeit, a confidence game, making something out of nothing at someone else's expense.

The danger, that is, is that there is nothing to trust backing it up. "In a world where only economic relations really matter," Gross says, ". . . all other values are eroded and distorted, and the real viable connections of community will not be present. For language not to be deceptive and obscuring, some sort of basis for trust must exist. If the 'circuit of speech' is only a vehicle for cynical self-interest, such trust is continually being destroyed. Language does not connect, it deceives, it controls, it manipulates. In a sense it can be said that real speech ceases to exist."

Whatever "the real viable connections of community" are, they are based on exchange. The haunting ambivalence Gross and most of the contributors here express towards money—and to a lesser extent towards fiction—is based on the fact that value seems to arise, like "interest," in and from exchange. As such, both money and fiction are liable to misuse, vehicles for distrust, yet they are among the most important currencies we have. But more than from misuse, the ambivalence towards money and language arises from the recognized possibility that value, whether embodied in fiction or in reserve notes, itself is illusory, metaphoric, only a quibble, interest on the absent principal of truth, reason, and propriety.

But maybe money, like fiction, can represent these things anyway. "The Candidate," Harris writes, "during all the first half-century of his life had thought of money as an item separate from virtue, but at last he was prepared to accept the idea of money as exchange." As such, it may approach virtue after all, create "virtue" in its exchange. This is the reason I quoted Gross at such length a moment ago: his statement is representative of the disturbing and disturbed ease with which discussions of money become discussions of language, literature, and the values they embody. This disturbing and easy exchange also yields interest—the illuminating understanding of these novels our essays offer is illusory "interest" perhaps, but in its own way it makes something important, as these essays do, out of the "naught" of fiction.

NOTES

1. Aristotle, *Politics*, trans. Benjamin Jowett (New York: Modern Library, 1943), p. 71.
2. *Preface to Shakespeare* in *Samuel Johnson: Rasselas, Poems and Selected Prose*, ed. Bertrand Bronson (New York, 1958), p. 252.
3. "On Truth and Lie in an Extra-Moral Sense" in *The Portable Nietzsche*, trans. and ed. Walter Kaufmann (New York, 1954), p. 47.

Money Talks

LITERATURE AND LUCRE: A Meditation

Leslie A. Fiedler
SUNY, Buffalo

It seems to me odd that I have never before, in my long life as a maker and teacher of fictions, talked from a public platform or written for publication about literature and lucre; and even odder that I feel so ill at ease attempting it for the first time. I am not suggesting that I do not ordinarily associate money with the arts I practice and for which I am these days more often than not paid. Indeed, I can scarcely separate the one from the other; since from the moment I was possessed (at age six or seven) by the desire to become a writer, I have been aware that the process—in our society at least—is inextricably involved with making money. Please understand. By "becoming a writer" I do not mean just getting out on to paper what I could no longer contain in my bursting heart and head, which is to fully consummated writing mere masturbation or *ejaculatio praecox*. What I yearned for was to be published, to be read, "to be great, to be known" (in the words of a poem by Stephen Spender which I have never forgotten), to open communication with an audience, to exist for others: utterly alien others, bound to me—unlike family or friends—only after the fact of having read me.

How hypothetical that audience, those alien others might remain, and consequently how unreal, impalpable the recognition, honor and love, I did not at first realize. To be sure, there are occasional letters of response, reviews in the press, even—if one lives long enough—testimonials and ceremonies. But for a long time, money (that one fiction of universal currency) is the only, and indeed always remains the most reliable, token that one has in fact touched, moved, shared one's most private fantasies with the faceless, nameless "you" to whom the writer's all-too-familiar "I" longs to be joined in mutual pleasure. "I stop somewhere waiting for you," is a sentence not just from Walt Whitman's but every writer's love letter to the world. It is only when the first royalty check arrives in the mail (an answer as palpable as a poem) that the writer begins to suspect that the "you" he has had to invent in his lonely chamber, in order to begin writing at all, is real; and that therefore his "I" (not the "I" to which like everyone else he is born, but that fictive "I" which he, in order to be a writer, must create simultaneously with the "you") is real, too.

But this means, as all writers know, though most of us (including me) find it hard to confess, that literature, the literary work, remains incomplete until it has passed from the desk to the market place; which is to say, until it has been packaged, huckstered, hyped and sold. Moreover, writers themselves (as they are also aware) remain reluctant virgins, crying to the world, "Love me! Love me!", until, as the revealing phrase of the trade has it, they have "sold their first piece." What scorn, therefore, the truly published, fully consummated writer has for those *demi-vierges* who publish themselves—turning in spinsterish despair to (again the customary phrase is significant) "Vanity Presses."

The fully published writer, however, feels not just scorn for the half-published and pity for the unpublished, but a kind of guilt, rather like the guilt of those who live by tourism or selling their own bodies. In his case as in theirs, that guilt breeds a kind of resentment against the intermediaries and accomplices who have made possible what he himself has desired. Just as the Western organizers of Rodeo Days hate dudes, or whores and gigolos their pimps, johns and aging benefactors, the commercially successful writer hates agents, editors, publishers, reviewers and the M.C.'s of T.V. Talk Shows—hates finally the poor audience itself for buying what has been offered for sale. That guilt and resentment I must admit I share, though by admitting it I compound my plight. But this surely is one of the reasons why, as I began by confessing, I feel ill at ease in approaching the subject so innocently proposed by the organizers of this symposium. I spoke the original version of this meditation in a setting which both symbolized and aggravated that guilt and resentment, since I had been paid to attend and testify; and I was present therefore, perhaps, not *just* for the sake of the lucre involved, but for that reason among others.

Indeed, I should like to think that the subject which I am treating is one so important to me and the community to which I belong that sooner or later I would have felt obliged to deal with it, even if somebody paid me *not* to do so. But this has not been my fate, so how can I be sure? In any case, here I am taking it up once more in print and for further payment, continuing communication much as I began it: not as one talks (or writes) to an old friend, or even to some one he sits beside on a plane, at a bar; but because there is a contract between us, because we are joined briefly by a cash nexus. In some sense, this, if not quite falsifies, at least uncomfortably modifies the nature of our discourse, creating real possibilities of distrust and misunderstanding. I have been paid to talk and write, while you have paid to listen and read. You, therefore, as you should, feel free, if I do not keep up my end of the bargain, neither entertain nor enlighten you, let's say, to grumble and complain: but *not*, in any case, to get your money back—not from me. It is a strange business, in which I am an entrepreneur, or rather a non-entrepreneur, guaranteed against risk.

But this is precisely the situation in which I have written and spoken for all of my professional life: as a novelist, poet, teacher, scholar and critic-pedagogue. Like other critic-pedagogues, I am not only paid for public performance; but I get free books for which other people pay hard cash, and am invited to attend without paying admission plays and movies for which others must buy tickets at the box-office. Moreover, I and my peers, or at least those among us who have access to commercial journals, are rewarded for a second time by being paid for registering in print our opinions of those books, movies and plays: opinions which *must* be (I sometimes uncomfortably suspect) radically different from the responses of those we address, precisely because having paid their way into the theatre, they have an investment to protect.

Even scholar-pedagogues who, out of a snobbishness desire to remain "pure," refuse to publish in paying journals like *The New York Times Book Review*, *The Times Literary Supplement* or, God forbid, *Esquire* and *Playboy* (in all of which, I must confess, I have appeared), cannot really escape the commercial trap. Unless willing to perish, they must publish *somewhere*; if only in subsidized journals of high prestige and low readability, like the *PMLA*, to which I have never contributed. But the readership of such journals consists not just of specialists in certain fields (unlike the readers of popular magazines, more inclined to disapprove than approve what they have paid for), but also the Promotion and Tenure committees of the Universities to which the contributors belong. Such committees will, on the basis of such articles, grant them tenure or promotion: thus guaranteeing that they will be paid more for repeating in the classroom what they have already published, or rehearsing what they hope to publish next. Eventually, moreover, such articles are gathered together, revised and expanded to make scholarly books, which have to be subsidized either by their authors or the schools in which they teach, since they are bought only by University Libraries, from whose shelves (a recent study has discovered) some seventy percent of them are *never* taken out.

Nonetheless, when these already over-subsidized pedagogues have persisted long enough in producing goods for which there is a reward but no market, they are likely to receive Grants and Fellowships, the most prestigious funded from carefully invested money, originally accumulated by Robber Barons like the Rockefellers, the Guggenheims and the Fords—which is to say, the filthiest American lucre of all. Furthermore, when they have attained seniority and prestige (or sometimes long before, while they are still only needy and promising) they may be asked to compile, collaborate in or merely lend their names to Freshman Texts. Carefully tailored to maximum classroom demand as determined by market analysts, such texts are the academic equivalents of blockbusting best-sellers by Jacqueline Susann, or Harold Robbins. Think, for instance, of Brooks' and Warren's inordinately successful *Understanding Poetry*, at once smugly elitist and happily profitable.

But is this not better, after all, than "selling out to Hollywood" like that backsliding Ivy League Professor, Erich Segal; or leaving the respectable sponsorship of Princeton University Press for the fleshpots of Simon and Schuster, who are not only the publishers of my own most recent book, but (I reassure myself) of Joseph Heller's *Catch-22*, a novel "taught" by some of my anti-commercial colleagues. Indeed, many, perhaps the great majority of the books taught by even the most snobbish and genteel among us were written by men shamelessly involved with the marketplace: Shakespeare, Richardson, Balzac, Dickens, Mark Twain, Scott Fitzgerald, Faulkner, Hemingway, Arthur Miller, Norman Mailer and Saul Bellow, to name only the first that come to mind. Moreover, in the last three or four decades, many writers we "require" in class have compounded their complicity by themselves becoming teachers, i.e., secondary as well as primary hucksters.

But, I remind myself, only a generation or two ago "serious" creative writers (the heirs of Modernist elitism and Marxist politics) considered employment in the univeristy—that front for what our own students were still calling in the sixties "the industrial-military complex"—a kind of "selling-out" comparable to taking a job with an advertising agency or MGM or Henry Luce: a search for low-level security in place of high-risk ventures in the arena of High Culture. Not in Grub Street, be it understood, but in Bohemia; that anti-Market Place, in which, after the invention of the Avant Garde and the raising of the slogan "*Epatez la bourgeoisie*," "true artists" were imagined as starving, while pseudoartists flourished.

Even in the hey-day of Modernism, the legend of *la vie de Bohème* did not deceive everyone. Sigmund Freud, for instance, remained faithful enough to the Reality Principle to argue that *all* artists were driven by fantasies of becoming beloved, famous and rich. And George Bernard Shaw, always the enemy of pious hypocrisy, ironically made the same point in his famous argument with Samuel Goldwyn over the filming of *My Fair Lady*, a musical based on his *Pygmalion*. "The trouble," he is reputed to have said, "is that you, Mr. Goldwyn, think about nothing but art, while all I think of is money." He is less likely to have been influenced by Freud, however, than by his true-blue English predecessor, Dr. Samuel Johnson, who is on record as believing that money is the "purest" of all motives for writing; by which I presume he meant it is the truest, the least likely to be mere cant and self-deceit. In any case, I remember both Shaw and Johnson each time I enter a group of strangers engaged in passionate debate, and discover that if they are discussing literature, nine times out of ten they turn out to be business men, but if they are talking about money, they are likely to be writers.

In America, however—perhaps precisely because among us commerce is officially more honored than art—our eminent writers have not typically spoken with equal candor on the subject of literature and lucre. Certainly, the great novelists of the mid-nineteenth century, celebrated in F.O. Matthiessen's *The American Renaissance* and D. H. Lawrence's *Studies in Classic American Literature*, have chosen self-pity over irony or frankness in talking about their relationship to the marketplace. The classic statement is Melville's, "Dollars damn me . . . all my books are botches. . . ." And implicit in this melancholy cry from the heart is a belief, as strong and pertinacious as any myth by which we live, that the authentic writer is neither drawn to nor confirmed in his vocation by the hope of marketplace success, the dream of becoming rich and famous; but can only be seduced by lucre, led to betray or prostitute his talent.

Paradoxically, American culture came of age at the very moment when old aristocratic sponsors of the arts were being replaced by the mass audience and the masters of the new media, who profit by responding to its taste. The first of these media was print, and the first truly popular genre, the Novel. But this is also the American form *par excellence*, invented even as we were inventing our Republic; and in it, the first American authors achieved fame for themselves and the culture which nurtured them. A commodity, mass produced and mass distributed, it offered its practitioners the possibility of growing rich as well as famous.

But from the start, that possibility remained more promise than fact, at least for writers like Charles Brockden Brown, Edgar Allan Poe, Nathaniel Hawthorne and Herman Melville, who thought of themselves as producing "literature."

Before the first of these sophisticated novelists (all male) had begun to write, "best sellers" were already being turned out by other more naive, less pretentious authors (largely female), whose taste and fantasy coincided with that of the popular audience, itself largely female. Even over the long haul, the books loved by most Americans who read anything between covers at all have not been *Moby Dick* and *The Scarlet Letter* nor even *Huckleberry Finn*, which live now chiefly as assigned reading in classrooms, but a series of deeply moving though stylistically undistinguished fictions, which begins with Susanna Rowson's *Charlotte Temple*, reaches a nineteenth-century high-point with Harriet Beecher Stowe's *Uncle Tom's Cabin* and a twentieth-century climax with Margaret Mitchell's *Gone with the Wind*. The last, though never approved by "serious" critics and seldom required in "serious" courses in literature, is still sold in paperback reprints; and, translated into the newer, more popular post-Gutenburg media of film and T.V., is probably known to a larger world-wide audience than any other American fiction.

For a century and a half, those writers among us who aspire to critical acclaim and an eternal place in libraries, have therefore felt compelled to struggle not just for their livelihood but for their very existence against the authors of "best sellers," whom they secretly envy and publicly despise. This cultural warfare may seem at first glance a struggle of the poor against the rich, the failed against the successful. But the situation is more complex than this since in terms of culture rather than economics, art novelists and their audience "fit though few" constitute a privileged, educationally-advantaged minority; while popular novelists and their mass readership remain a despised *lumpen* minority, whose cultural insecurity is further shaken when their kids learn in school to question their taste.

The struggle of High Art and Low is, moreover, a battle of the sexes. Referring to the writers who had preempted the paying audience before he ever entered the scene, Nathaniel Hawthorne called them a "damn'd mob of scribbling women." And, indeed, from Mrs. Rowson to Jacqueline Susann, the authors of monumental, long-lasting popular successes have continued to come from the sex which thinks of itself as otherwise exploited, oppressed, dominated in a patriarchal society.

Unlike other oppressive minorities, however (white slave owners, for example), it is possible for both males and the cultural elite to contend, with a certain superficial plausibility, that they are victims rather than victimizers. And, indeed, both primary and secondary literature in the United States, the novels and poems of which we are most proud and the critical/autobiographical works written on them, reflect the myth of the "serious" writer as an alienated male, condemned to neglect and poverty by a culture simultaneously commercialized and feminized.

There are prototypes of this myth in remotest antiquity: the legend of Euripides, for instance, first avant-garde artist in the West, having been hunted to death by a pack of angry women (or, alternatively, dogs); while behind even that is the primal image of Dionysus, torn to pieces by Bacchantes, eager to still his singing and exact revenge for their slighted sex. It is Poe, however, who first embodies that image for the American imagination, at least as he has been re-interpreted for us by French poets of the *décadence*, Baudelaire and Mallarmé, who celebrated him as a *poète maudit*, "*un Byron egaré dans le nouveau monde.*" But even earlier, Poe had collaborated, as it were, with his friend-enemy Rufus Griswold to create a demi-fictional portrait of himself as a dope-ridden alcoholic, dying in the streets of Baltimore after a long starvation and neglect in an environment hostile to art.

That image of the true artist destroyed by a money-grubbing society, though originally the hybrid offspring of Southern American self-hated and the French contempt for everything in our culture except its presumed victims, throve in the New World. Reembodied generation after generation, it is most notably exemplified after Poe by Herman Melville, whom we rejoice to imagine drudging away his last unhappy years in the Custom House, unpublished, unhonored, forgotten; and Scott Fitzgerald, dying in shabby surroundings in a Hollywood which preferred Mammon to literature, and had no sense that this failed alcoholic scriptwriter was destined to outlive in glory the most celebrated producers, directors and actors of his time. That Poe and Melville and Fitzgerald failed not because they despised lucre and shunned the marketplace, but precisely because they were so desperately committed to the American dream of "making it," the legend does not permit us to remember.

We really know that Fitzgerald began by producing best-selling novels and peddling hastily written short stories to family magazines at prices which mounted with his fame; and that he ended by squandering away a larger fortune than ordinary Americans can imagine earning in a lifetime of backbreaking work. Poe, too, though never as successful, even momentarily, spent his brief career as a hack-writer and editor of commercial literary journals in pursuit of the common reader and the quick buck. Indeed, the fantasies which drove them both are betrayed in stories like Poe's "The Gold-Bug" and Fitzgerald's "A Diamond as Big as the Ritz"—the dream of innocently acquiring guilty treasure, and the nightmare of losing everything.

Similarly, the mad, metaphysical quest of Melville's *Moby Dick* begins as a carefully planned commercial venture, with Ishmael bargaining for his fair share of the profits. And why not—in light of the fact that Melville's mad, metaphysical career began with the best seller, *Typee*. Indeed, he never ceased trying to recapture his initial rapport with the popular audience. Even *Pierre*, whose underlying theme is the plight of the alienated artist in America, he assured his publisher (and perhaps believed himself) was "a rural bowl of milk," i.e., a domestic romance as palatable to the large female audience as to the somewhat smaller male one who had admired his adventure stories.

The pathos of such writers, whether they ended in insanity and withdrawal like Melville or in premature death like Poe and Fitzgerald, is not that they nobly refused to provide what the marketplace demanded, but that they tried to do so and failed. But this is not the story which the American mass audience likes to be told, since they need to be assured that the writers they choose only posthumously to honor (if not read) in some sense died for their sins: their lack of sensibility, mindless pursuit of profit, indifference to art—but not to artists, particularly failed ones, after they are dead. Realizing how in our world nothing succeeds like failure—certain lesser writers, from Rufus Griswold to Budd Schulberg, have produced parasitic best sellers about the tragic fates of Poe and Fitzgerald.

It may have been booze that destroyed Poe or Fitzgerald, but the great public prefers to believe they did it with their little hatchets—thus feeling at once powerful and guilty: a potent emotional mix for all true Americans. Certainly, we do not seem to derive as much satisfaction from contemplating the careers of eminent writers who have made it, dying, like Harriet Beecher Stowe, honored and rich—though cheerfully batty. It is, for instance, Mark Twain's final loneliness and melancholia we prefer to dwell on, or his many failures along the way. Yet though Twain went bankrupt as often as any other capitalist entrepreneur of the Gilded Age, at the end he was able to support a splendiferous house, and a set of bad habits which compelled him to smoke forty Havana cigars a day and to drink enough Old Grandad to send him to bed insensible night after night. He had finally grown so wealthy, indeed, that the only people he felt he could talk to as equals were Henry Rogers, Vice President of Standard Oil, and Andrew Carnegie, whom he addressed as "St. Andrew" in letters signed "St. Mark."

Ironically, his fortune was based on the continuing success of *Huckleberry Finn*, which is to say, the classic version of the American anti-success story. We are asked to love Huck (and to prove our love by buying the book in which he appears) for running away, not just from school, church and family, but money as well: that guilty-innocent treasure which he and Tom had stumbled on at the end of *Tom Sawyer*, but which he, unlike Tom and the hero of Poe's "The Gold Bug," ultimately rejects. What Twain never wrote was a fictional account of a boy like himself, who, instead of "lighting out for the territory ahead of the rest," stayed home, grew up (as he would not let Tom grow up), permitted himself to be "civilized" by his wife and daughter; and at last got rich by writing about another eternal child who made all the opposite choices. Before the middle of the twentieth century, in fact, there is no respectable American book which portrays sympathetically an author who made good. Even Horatio Alger's disreputable juveniles, though they portray striking it rich as a truly Happy Ending, deal with boys who rose from rags to riches by becoming not writers but merchants or bankers.

Only in the last decade of this century did it become possible, first in fact, then in fiction, for a novelist highly regarded by critics (Norman Mailer is an example) to become wealthy long before his death by having his books chosen as major Book Club Selections; then signing million dollar paperback contracts; and finally appearing on T.V. Talk Shows, where (becoming, as it were, his own Griswold or Schulberg) he played the mythological role of the writer for the benefit of an audience which had not read, never would read his work. Even novelists who shun all publicity, like J. D. Salinger and Thomas Pynchon, accumulate royalties comparable to those earned by such critically despised darlings of the populace as Harold Robbins and Jacqueline Susan. Only Saul Bellow, however, Nobel Prize Winner and Laureate of the New Conservatism, has thus far dared translate this new-style Happy Ending from life to literature. And this is perhaps why his *Humboldt's Gift* has been universally (willfully, I suspect) misunderstood by its critics.

It seems, at first, a rather conventional elegy for a *poète maudit*: the last, somewhat improbable heir to the tradition of Poe, Melville and Fitzgerald, reborn this time as a failed New York Jewish intellectual—a super-articulate, self-defeating *luftmensch*, who has died abandoned and penniless before the action of the novel begins. It has been suggested by many, including Bellow himself, that the model for Humboldt was the poet, Delmore Schwartz, who had indeed come to such a shabby end. But while there is a great deal of Schwartz in Humboldt, he is finally the portrait not of any single individual but of a whole generation of Jewish-American losers: including, surely, Bellow's one-time guru and life-long friend, Issac Rosenfeld, also dead before reaching forty, his handful of stories and essays remembered by a shrinking handful of aging admirers; and perhaps Lenny Bruce as well, that hipster and stand-up comedian who O.D.'d in 1966. Reading of Humboldt's fate, I cannot, in any case, help thinking of *all* those mad, bright young Jewish Americans, still caught up in the obsolescent myth of the Artist as Victim, and dead before they had lived long enough to realize, like Bellow, that in prosperous America it was no longer necessary to end as a Beautiful Loser.

In any case, Bellow's book is called not *Humboldt* but *Humboldt's Gift*; and the recipient of that gift, that not-so-beautiful Winner, Charlie Citrine, is its real hero. For a little while, Citrine (who at times seems scarcely distinguishable from his author) finds in Humboldt's death and his own survival, an occasion for guilt—the guilt we have long been trained to think of as the inevitable accompaniment of making it. But in the end, he succeeds in convincing himself that Humboldt has died for him, that all such losers die for all winners; leaving us as a heritage not empty regrets but a saleable story: his story once, our story now, the book we are reading. Properly exploited, that story can (in the fiction we read) be sold to the movies, or (in the larger world outside) clinch for its author the Nobel Prize; make us survivors, in short, rich enough to meet the obligations of the prosperous living: alimony, mortgage payments, credit card debits, fifty percent income taxes. And if we weep a little, remembering those others whom we loved and betrayed and by whose death we profited, we can (as the old saying has it) cry all the way to the bank.

The Gold Bug
Marc Shell
SUNY, Buffalo

i The Bug for Gold

At a time when alchemists were trying to transform tin into gold by means of alchemy and financiers were turning paper into gold by means of the newly widespread institution of paper money Edgar Allan Poe was a poor author who could only wish to exchange his literary papers for money. Among these papers were those that compose "The Gold-Bug" (1843), a popular tale that tells how a character (Legrand, an impoverished Southern aristocrat with many resemblances to Poe himself) used his intellect to decipher a paper and thus find gold.[1]

Money, in the sense of treasure, is a main "theme" of the story. "The intent of the author," wrote one reviewer in 1845, "was evidently to write a popular tale: money, and the finding of money being chosen as the most popular thesis."[2] Poe knew the popularity of the theme. He wrote in 1841 that "a main source of the interest which [Samuel Warren's *Ten Thousand a Year*] possesses for the mass, is to be referred to the pecuniary nature of its theme . . . it is an affair of pounds, shillings and pence."[3]

In "The Gold-Bug" the narrator and Legrand remark on the hundreds of histories and stories about "money-diggers" (pp. 822, 833–34).[4] "The Gold-Bug" itself is a story like these others, but with certain differences. For example, as Legrand points out, in "The Gold-Bug" the gold-seekers become gold-finders, which was not the usual *topos*. Moreover, although the ostensible theme of "The Gold-Bug" is the search for money in the sense of treasure, its actual thesis and mode of presentation suggest, as we shall see, a concern with money as currency and with paper money in particular as a unique sort of redeemable symbol. Thus the theme of treasure is internalized in the narration and its symbols. This study of "The Gold-Bug" is an interpretation of the interiorization of one economic form—the one associated with paper money—into a work of literature.

ii "Gold-bug? Humbug!"

> We have no hesitation in stating the fact, that *humbug* beyond all question is at last the "Philosopher's stone," in the discovery of which so many geniuses have heretofore been bewildered.
> —Review of "The Gold-Bug" signed by "D"

Entomological Specimen

The bug that causes "gold fever" in "The Gold-Bug" has been classified by literary critics as though it were a specimen of beetle for entomological investigation.[5] It has been categorized in the same way that one would classify a tarantula such as the one mentioned in the epigraph to "The Gold-Bug":

> What ho! what ho! this fellow is dancing mad!
> He hath been bitten by the Tarantula.
> —*All in the Wrong*[6]

Legrand, a great collector of "entomological specimens" (p. 807), with, no doubt, a large "cabinet" (p. 813), is himself at first an entomological classifier, and he gives many critics their first misleading lead.

The entomological critics collect and name different specimens of beetles from Sullivan Island (where "The Gold-Bug" takes place), and consider the relationship of the gold bug in Poe's story to the beetles discussed in the *Natural History* which Poe helped to edit.[7] They are like Legrand in his first catalogical researches in entomology, conchology (pp. 807, 808), botany, and even numismatics (the narrator calls coins and counters "specimens" [p. 827] hitherto unseen by them).[8] The specificity of description in Poe's style requires such knowledge as these classifying sciences offer. (Baudelaire pointed this out with reference to the catalogue of coins in the treasure trove.)[9] Yet this categorization into species is ultimately debunked in "The Gold-Bug": Legrand comes to regard such classification as one of several pieces of "mystification" (cf. p. 844). The self-dubbed "bug men" believe that "the whole bug is not a pure figment of the imagination,"[10] but we shall see that it is ultimately associable with a "thing which is not."

Species of Madness

The bug has also been classified as though it were a species of madness for psychological investigation. It has been categorized in the same way that one would classify the disease that the spider is said to cause—the dance of the Tarantula.

"The Gold-Bug" does present an interesting case study for psychoanalysts. They might, for example, classify the gold bug as a species of *Dukatenschiesser* (dung-beetle, or "shitter of ducats"), seeming to follow here the investigations of the bug men. They then might make the typical Freudian association of shiny metal with faeces or of lucre with filth.[11] "Bug" means "madman,"[12] and the psychoanalytic interpretation might tend to classify the particular species of madness from which Legrand and presumably also Poe suffer. By following such an analysis they might connect lucre with the imagination, which is a major aesthetic concern in "The Gold-Bug."

But as Legrand had already beaten the entomological critics to the method of classifying insects, so he has beaten the psychological ones (including, perhaps, the narrator) to the method of classifying madnesses (including his own). He notes that "the mind struggles to establish a connexion—a sequence of cause and effect—and being unable to do so, suffers a species of temporary paralysis" (p. 829). The tale itself constitutes, as we shall see, an implicit critique of the kind of classification and deciphering of evidence—Poe's text and Poe himself—in which both psychology and entomology engage.

The Humbug and the Specie

Ultimately the gold bug is a tricky symbol that debunks ordinary classification of both physical and mental things. It is similar to the riddling bug in Poe's "The Sphinx," in which a bug that seemed to be enormous turns out to be inconsequentially small. It is like the "confidence man of merchandise" who is described in the *Literary World* (1849) as a "new species of the Jeremy Diddler."[13] The gold-bug is a humbug.

This term, "humbug," appears frequently in the first literary criticism of "The Gold-Bug." This was a debate in 1843 about the monetary circumstances surrounding the publication of "The Gold-Bug" and the way that it was cashed in for gold. Poe first sent his story to *Graham's*, and was paid fifty-two dollars for it. He then withdrew his work in order to enter it in a contest with a prize of one hundred dollars which was being held by the *Dollar Newspaper*. Poe was wise thus to bank on his work. "The Gold-Bug" won first prize. (The second prize was awarded to Robert Morris's *The Banker's Daughter*.)[14] Contemporary reviewers suspected fraud in the payment of one hundred dollars by the *Dollar Newspaper* for a tale about the search for dollars. In "The 'Gold-Bug'—a Decided Humbug" (1843), for example, a certain "D" wrote that "the publisher [of the *Dollar*] announce[d] with a grand flourish the literary tournament, and . . . induce[d] a number of really meritorious writers to enter the lists and compete for the nominal prize, which ha[d] all the appearance at first of a "Gold Bug," but . . . certain[ly] eventuate[d] in a humbug." "D" accused the contest and the tale itself of being a "literary *humbug*." There was an ensuing public controversy in which "D" and one "Mr. P" (probably Poe) confronted each other in the matter of "the prize story."[15] The discussion of the external economics of "The Gold-Bug" (Poe's winning the contest) came to illuminate for some readers its internal economics (Legrand's apparently using a gold bug designed on paper to find gold). The external and internal economics of the tale thus came together.[16]

But what is this humbug in "The Gold-Bug?" A humbug is a thing that is not. Ontology, or the logic of being and substance, may help locate the logical place of the gold bug in "The Gold-Bug." Poe's contemporaries called for a new study of the connections between ontology and political economy. Such a study would shed light on the connection in "The Gold-Bug" between species in the physical world (including entomological ones) and species in the internal world of the mind (including psychological ones), a connection that links nature with the psyche, or things with our ideas of them. It is no accident, as we shall see, that Legrand's search for natural specimens and his study of different psychological species turns into a search for metallic "specie." The turn from species and specimens to specie is a crucial articulation in "The Gold-Bug," which Poe wrote when the main public forum for discussing the relationship between symbols and things was the ideological debate about how, if at all, paper money and coined money represent substantial things such as gold.

iii Paper Against Gold: Monetary and Aesthetic Theory

> It has always been one of the arts of [U.S.] federalism to address itself most strongly to human cupidity, as though sordid interest was the controlling influence which actuates mankind. During Jefferson's [Democratic Republican] administration foreign rapacity was defended [by the Federalists], and he was falsely charged with producing the commercial embarrassments which existed. And while the country was afterwards struggling in a sanguinary conflict with a powerful enemy, the leaders of this party [Harrison of the Federalists, for example], regardless of the liberty and independence of the Republic, sighed aloud in lugubrious tones, for "the *golden* days of commer-

cial prosperity." The same false charges are now made against the present administration of the general government [that of the Democratic Republican Van Buren], and the same tones are now loudly uttered with the variation only of a single word, occasioned by the modern whig [Federalist] discovery that gold is a "humbug" and *paper* is therefore substituted for "*golden*."

—Samuel Young, "Oration Delivered at the Democratic Republican Celebration of the 64th Anniversary of the Independence of the United States," July Fourth, 1840

America was the historical birthplace of widespread paper money in the Western World,[17] and a debate about coined and paper money dominated American political discourse from 1825 to 1845. The "paper money men" (as the advocates of paper money were called) were versed against the "gold bugs" (as the advocates of gold against paper money were called, and also the advocates of a gold against a silver standard).[18] Books, such as William Cobbett's long treatise, *Paper Against Gold*, made plenty of both gold and paper money.

The paper money debate was concerned with symbolization in general, and hence not only with money but also with aesthetics. Symbolization in this context concerns the relationship between the substantial thing and its sign. Solid gold (from which the ingots of gold coin were made) was associated with the substance of value. Whether one regarded paper as an appropriate symbol (as did "paper money men") or as an inappropriate and downright misleading one (as did "gold bugs"), that sign was "insubstantial" insofar as the paper counted for nothing as a commodity and was thus "insensible" in the economic system of exchange.

The paper of money was called an appearance or shadow. Plate 1, a cartoon entitled "A Shadow is not a Substance," depicts the relationship between substance and shadow—paper monies were called "Greenbacks"—which some thinkers believed to obtain not only in monetary but also in aesthetic representation (not only, that is, in the humbug that Samuel Young called paper money but also in the humbug that "D" called "The Gold-Bug" and its gold bug).[19] That this purported relationship between reality and appearance is both monetary and aesthetic helps to explain many poets' and economists' association of paper money with ghostliness,[20] and Jupiter's association in "The Gold-Bug" of gold with ghost (or of "goul," as he puts it, with "gose" [p. 812]).[21]

A SHADOW IS NOT A SUBSTANCE.

PLATE I

THE GOLD BUG

MILK-TICKETS FOR BABIES, IN PLACE OF MILK.

PLATE II

In America, comparisons were made between the way a mere shadow or piece of paper becomes credited as substantial money and the way that an artistic appearance is taken for the real thing by a willing suspension of disbelief. (The tale "The Gold-Bug," and the design of a gold bug on paper which "The Gold-Bug" describes, are both works of art which are exchanged for and hence to be taken for gold.) Congress, it was said, could turn paper into gold by an "act of congress" that makes it money. Why could not an artist turn paper with a gold bug designed on it into gold? Thus a humorous American cartoon shows one paper with a cow designed on it and the inscription, "This is a cow by the act of the artist," and another paper which reads "This is money by the act of congress" (Plate II).

Understanding the relationship between substance and sign was complicated by the known existence and practical monetary validity of counterfeit notes (i.e., illegal copies of legitimate ghost monies) and, more significant for understanding movements such as American Symbolism, of phantom bank-notes. "There were no real banks, no officers, or actual assets of any kind to make these notes by 'phantom' banks of any real value,—except the ability to 'pass' them on some unsuspecting person."[22] These papers—with their designs, insignia, signatures and even ciphers as fictional as the ones that Poe imagines for Kidd's memorandum or index—passed for ghost money and hence for solid specie. Even the "bank note reporters" and "counterfeit detectors"—the critics in the fray—could be counterfeited or entirely fabricated by confidence men.[23] Phantoms, counterfeit ghosts, and ghosts passed all alike.

The fear that all literature was, like money, in this sense, a merely passable "naught"—a mere cipher—troubled Melville, an expert on confidence, for whom the tropic center of symbolization is an "algebraic x" threatening language and money with devaluation and annihilation.[24] Credit or belief involves the very ground of aesthetic experience, and the same medium that seems to confer it in fiduciary money (bank-notes) and in scriptural money (created by the process of bookkeeping) also seems to confer it in literature. That medium is writing. The apparently "diabolical" "interplay of money and mere writing to a point where the two be[come] confused"[25] involves a general ideological development: the tendency of paper money to distort our "natural" understanding of the relationship between symbols and things. The sign of the monetary diabolus, which many Americans insisted was like the one that God impressed in Cain's forehead,[26] condemns men to misunderstand the world of symbols and things in which they live.

This debate in aesthetics and economics, with its large political dimensions, seemed to require a new kind of study of money together with other kinds of symbols. Thus Clinton Roosevelt, a prominent member of the Loco-Focos, argued in his "Paradox of Political Economy" in 1859, when Van Buren (advocate for gold) had lost the presidency, that the American Association for the Advancement of Science should establish an "*ontological department* for the discussion and establishment of general principles of political economy."[27] (In Germany, such an ontological discussion already existed in the shape of a far-ranging debate between the proponents of idealism and the proponents of realism.)[28]

Poe did not enter directly into the debate about paper money. Of course, he did make many pronouncements about wealth and cupidity.[29] He did associate with John L. O'Sullivan's *Democratic Review*, and he called Richard Adams Locke—who contributed to the *New Era* which attacked paper money—"one of the few men of *unquestionable* genius whom the country possesses."[30] And some of his stories—"King Pest," for example—can be interpreted to be allegorical burlesques of Jackson's and Van Buren's monetary policy much like *Quodlibet* (1840), the political satire by Poe's friend John Pendleton Kennedy.[31] Nevertheless, it would be wrong to say that Poe was either a Federalist or a Democratic Republican where matters of gold and paper were concerned. "The Gold-Bug" is not so much concerned with problems of monetary policy as with the implicit relationship between aesthetic symbolization and paper money symbolization.

iv From Nothing to Something

We humans sometimes make mountains out of molehills. But only God and his opposite number can make something out of nothing. Maybe alchemists can make gold out of tin, but they cannot make tin out of what Jupiter calls "no tin." For us the terrible dictum—that nothin' will come of nothin'[32]—seems to hold true. Except, that is, in the shadowy realms of aesthetics and monetary policy.

One interpreter argues that from the alchemical point of view Legrand does not discover but actually generates or (re)produces the gold in the hole. "It is actually Legrand's Romantic imagination that helps to accomplish the multiplication of the gold-bug into Captain Kidd's treasure."[33] Legrand himself notes that "there seemed to glimmer, faintly within the most remote and secret chambers of my intellect, a glow-worm-like conception of that truth which last night's adventure [unearthing the gold] brought so magnificent a demonstration" (p. 829). This generative power of the intellect which Legrand associates with a psychic entomoid—the intellectual glow-worm that is the humbug of the tale—is closely linked with financial institutions that render treasure from paper.

Since Aristotle, finance has been accused of making something out of nothing or out of nothing natural.[34] Aristotle was concerned with the way that coined money was made to breed by usury, but Poe and his contemporaries were concerned with the subversive manner of representation and exchange in the institution of paper money in particular. The immediate distinction between coin and paper money can be expressed in terms of the relationship between an ingot and an inscription on it when both together compose a coin. This relationship of sign or symbol (the inscription) to substance (the ingot) is the heart of the aesthetic version of the paper money debate. There are two related questions here. First: when the inscription disappears from the surface of a coin, is the remaining ingot still a coin? In his numismatic catalogue the narrator mentions "coins so worn that we [can] make nothing of their inscription" (p. 827). This "nothing" that we can make of their inscriptions does not make the ingots into "things which are not." However much they may lose their status as coins, they are still substantial metal commodities. Second: when the ingot itself disappears, and all that remains is the inscription, the literature, is the numismatic inscription still substantially valid as is symbolic paper money? Can the shadow that is paper money thus become as valuable as, or even more valuable than the substance that is specie? The narrator in Nathaniel Hawthorne's "The Seven Vagabonds" (1842) suggests as much when he gives a beggar a five dollar bill with the claim that "it is a bill of the Suffolk Bank . . . and better than the specie."[35]

Symbol and Thing as Cause and Effect

> Since fortune has thought fit to bestow [the bug] upon me, I have only to use it properly and I shall arrive at the gold of which it is the index. (p. 815)

The design of the gold bug, like the bug itself, is to be considered initially as a cause of the treasure which has a metonymic link to it, and then, less grandly, as a symbolic counterpart to or index of Captain Kidd's cartograph. Legrand is like both Midas and Pygmalion in his reaction to the design of the bug: he seems to believe that he can turn his "graphic" art (p. 828), of which he is tolerably proud, into the real thing. He would transform his design of a specimen into specie, thus treating the designed paper as a necessary cause of an effect—the unearthing of gold—that he seeks.

The distinction of accidental from necessary relationships both between signs and substance and between one event and another is a major theoretical problem in "The Gold-Bug," as in most detective stories, and Legrand eventually comes to address it. Is the connection between the design of the gold bug and the gold, for example, merely accidental? That is, are they linked in the same way as two meanings connected by punning (Captain Kidd with the kid in the hieroglyphic signature), by malapropism (Jupiter's "goul" with "gold"), and by homonymity (the design of the bug with the pirate's insignium—both called "death's heads")?[36] Are they linked, that is, in the same way as the coincidences in the plot—Legrand and the narrator call them links in a chain of happy accidents—such as the "fortuitous" entrance of the dog from the cold outdoors?[37] Or is the connection between signs and substance and also between one event and another somehow natural or logically necessary rather than accidental? That is, are they linked in the same way as words with things in onomatopoeia ("hum" with the sound of humming)[38] or as an animal with its native territory (an eagle, for example, with the United States)?[39]

In implicitly considering these questions, Poe integrates into his tale contemporary problems involving money and aesthetics. In the cartoon entitled "A Shadow is not a Substance," for example, the specie can be viewed as one cause of the shadow. The specie and the sun are two links in the chain of cause and effect which a detective might say produces the shadow. In "The Gold-Bug" the events in the plot and the eventual discovery of gold are not connected by this kind of necessity. To say that the design of the gold bug on the paper is a link in a chain of symbols or events which leads inevitably to the gold is, adopting the terms of the caricature, to say that the shadow is the cause of the substance rather than vice versa. According to the "gold bugs," this is the ostensibly absurd position of the "paper money men," of whom Legrand seems to be one as he marches through the dark forest with the designed paper clutched in his hand.

And yet, however absurd, the bug and the original design of the bug do lead somehow to the insignium and signature on Captain Kidd's valuable paper, and even, as the narrator remarks, to "a letter between the stamp and the signature," or, as Legrand himself says, to "the text for these contexts" (p. 833).

Species of Cryptograph

The text of Kidd's paper is a cryptic cartograph in alphabetic cipher. Those critics who attack Poe for his supposedly inaccurate knowledge of ciphering and cryptography are mistaken in their criticism or miss the point of the story.[40] First, these critics do not seem to know that a common form of cipher writing in the United States was the literary genre of paper money inscriptions, into which "errors" were often purposefully incorporated in order to trap counterfeiters more easily.[41] Second, the cryptological critics fall into the same interpretative trap as the entomological and psychoanalytical ones. Deciphering the secret-writing of the parchment and hence connecting sign with substance, as Legrand goes about doing it, is identical in method to the cataloguing of species involved in these and similar "exact" sciences. "Be assured," says Legrand, "that the *specimen* before us appertains to the very simplest *species* of cryptograph" (839, cf. p. 835). Legrand's deciphering the cipher on the parchment stands as a warning to those who would similarly decipher the book (Hebrew *sēpher*) that is "The Gold-Bug," whose center is a real cipher (Arabic *ziffre*, or "O") quite mystified and mystifying.

v The Goolah Bug: Linguistic Goolah and Monetary Goole

Language and Money

The distinction between substance and shadow in monetary and aesthetic theory affects the understanding of symbolization in general and of linguistic representation in particular. With the advent of paper money certain analogies, such as the one that "paper is to gold as word is to meaning," came to exemplify and to inform logically the discourse about language. For example, a call was made by critics for a return to gold not only in money but also in aesthetics and language. Thus Emerson wrote that "a man's power to connect his thought with its proper symbol, and so to utter it" is corrupted when "new imagery ceases to be created, and old words are perverted to stand for things which are not; a paper currency is employed, when there is no bullion in the vaults."[42]

As Emerson suggests, paper money differs from coined money in an intellectually suggestive way.[43] While a coin may be both symbol (as inscription or type) and commodity (as metallic ingot), paper is only (or virtually all) symbolic. Thus Wittgenstein chooses to compare meaningless sounds with scraps of paper rather than with unminted ingots. Or, to put it the other way, he compares meaningful words with valuable paper money rather than with coins.[44] In "The Gold-Bug," what in the intellect or in the imagination of Legrand creates gold is like what turns paper into a valuable commodity.

For the same reason as Wittgenstein, Marx distinguishes the disassociation of symbol from commodity that seems to occur in the minting of metal ingots into coin, from the less apparent and ideologically more subversive disassociation of symbol from commodity that occurs in printing money. As Marx argues, credit money (the extreme form of paper money) divorces the "name" entirely from what it is supposed to represent and so seems to allow an "idealist" transcendence or conceptual annihilation of commodities.[45]

In the institution of paper money, sign and substance—paper and gold—are clearly disassociated, much as word is disassociated from meaning in punning.

Discourse "By Jupiter!"

In "The Gold-Bug," the malapropian and punning speech of the manumitted black slave is as important to our deciphering the meaning of the tale as his scythe was to Legrand's getting at the gold. "It would have been impossible, to force our way but for the scythe and Jupiter" (p. 817). Jupiter's dialect, which students of linguistics call "Goolah," is in this sense the real "goole" in "The Gold-Bug."[46]

Goolah was a linguistic dialect spoken by blacks living on the sea islands and tidewater coastal strip bordering South Carolina. There are instances in "The Gold Bug" where Poe seems to depart from Goolah,[47] and there is unnecessary eye-dialect in the tale: not only the sound (as in ear-dialect)[48] but also the spelling is incorrect according to standard White American usage. (Jupiter's "syphon" [p. 912], for example, is eye-dialect for "ciph'n," which is ear-dialect or malapropism for "deciphering.") Jupiter's apparent inconsistencies ("no tin"/"noffin"/ "notin"), however, tend to illuminate the central thesis of the tale, which concerns not so much money as treasure, as paper money as a sign with no necessary relation to its referent. Jupiter's language depends for its interpretational effectiveness on accidental connections between words and meanings. The difficulty of connecting words with their meaningful "origins" is most extreme in the case of Goolah. A Virginian journalist wrote in 1838 that "the etymology of [several] terms is quite untraceable as that of any terms in the Goolah . . . dialect."[49]

Jupiter's discourse provides an interpretative access to the discontinuity in the symbolization and plot of "The Gold-Bug." For example, the bug that is described by Legrand at first in entomological terms as having "antennae," is redefined by Jupiter as rather having "no *tin* in him" (pp. 808–09).[50] Poe's making Jupiter pun on "no tin" has been attacked as "stupid" by several critics who fail to note the literary and economic status of the pun.[51] What could the pun mean? First, there was "no tin" in the bug (which would be important for alchemical interpretation) so that it was of "real gold" or "solid gold" (pp. 809, 815, 833). Second, there was "no thing" inside the bug, so that it was hollow in the physical sense. Third, there was "nothing" in the bug, that is, "nothing" to it. If there were nothing to the bug, it would be a cipher, an insubstantial ghost that might, like paper money, indicate something substantial.

In "The Gold-Bug" Goolah connects by verbal punning other threads of the story. For example, Jupiter's version of "goole-bug" tends to illuminate the connections or disconnections between devil, gold, and God: the devil is heard or seen in "goul";[52] gold in "goole"; and God in "my golly" (p. 824) and "Lor-gol-a-marcy" (p. 820).

Goolah also serves to make clearer aspects of the paper money men's quest to become rich by manipulation of paper money ghosts. Jupiter's "gose" (p. 812), for example, can be interpreted in three ways: as "ghost," which refers to banknotes; as the "goose" or person "gulled" into accepting counterfeit ghosts or phantom banknotes in the belief that they are good as "gold"; and as the design of a "goose" which appeared on American banknotes.[53]

In "The Gold-Bug" Poe thus shows interest in a generation of something from nothing that is at once economic and linguistic. He took his studies of the "omnipotence of money" and of usury—themes that he praised in *Tortesa the Usurer* (1839), which he called the greatest play by an American[54]—and transformed them, on the one hand, into a story about the generation of gold from a bug or from a design of a bug, and on the other hand, into discourse whose exemplary means of generating meaning is Goolah punning.

Aristotle argues that of all forms of generation usury is the most unnatural, and theorists since the medieval era have argued that punning is its linguistic counterpart, since punning makes an unnatural, even a diabolical, supplement of meaning from a sound that is properly attached to only one (if any) meaning.[55] Thus, in terms of the economics of symbolization in "The Gold-Bug," Goolah is the linguistic counterpart to the productive imagination of Legrand, a counterpart that is its symptomatic externalization, since Jupiter's language is there for us to see and to hear.

vi The Last Words

"Seekers after gold dig up much earth and find little."[56] Heraclitus warns that the search for gold, for meaning, is a kind of misdirected bugaboo. There is something cryptic and disconcerting about the conclusion to "The Gold Bug." Legrand's cryptography is successful, but the unearthing of the secreted coffer reveals coffinless skeletons in the crypt-like hole. "What are we to make of the skeletons found in the hole?" the narrator asks Legrand (p. 844). This is an unanswered question in a detective story that only seems to answer all questions.[57] "Who shall tell?" are the last words in "The Gold-Bug."

"The Gold-Bug" is a tale in which an impoverished aristocrat, who "saunters along the bank in quest of entomological specimens" (p. 807) discovers there a paper that renders forth golden specie most of which is exchanged at the bank for commercial papers.[58] What began at a bank also ends at one. It is not ashes to ashes and dust to dust, as for the ghostly men whose remains are skeletons, but rather paper to paper. The treasure itself returns to the bank where, so to speak, it originated. It is as though it were a thing that was naught at all.

NOTES

1. Poe derided attempts to get rich quick. His tale "Von Kempelen and his Discovery" mocks alchemy, for example, and as Harry Levin argues (*The Power of Blackness: Hawthorne, Poe, Melville* [New York, 1964], esp. pp. 138–39), Poe "was to take a dim view of the California Gold Rush [of 1949] in the poem [El Dorado], and to argue that the success of alchemy would deflate the value of ore." Yet Poe regarded himself as a Virginia gentleman and once was disappointed in his expectation of being heir to one of the wealthiest men in Richmond (Ernest Marchand, "Poe as a Social Critic," *AL*, 6 [1934–35], 42–43; J. W. Krutch, *Edgar Allan Poe* [New York, 1926], Chapter 2; Hervey Allen, *Israfel: The Life and Times of Edgar Allan Poe*, 2 vols. [New York, 1926], vol. I, 116; and *The Complete Works of Edgar Allan Poe*, Virginia Edition, 17 vols. [New York, 1902], vol. XVII, 15).

Alexis de Tocqueville indicated the literary milieu in which Poe worked in a chapter of his *Democracy in America* (1835–40) entitled "The Industry of Letters." In that industry Poe was not, as Charles Baudelaire noted, a "money-making author" (Charles Baudelaire, "Edgar Allan Poe: Sa Vie et ses Ouvrages," in *Charles Baudelaire: Oeuvres completes*, ed. Yves Florenne [Paris, 1966], p. 8). Baudelaire complains that Poe's American biographers often criticized him for not having made more money, and he explains that Poe wrote "too much above the common intellectual level for him to be well paid" (Baudelaire, p. 23).

2. Thomas Dunn English, *Aristidean* (October, 1845). In an edition of "The Gold-Bug" for sixth-grade students, Theda Gildemeister suggests that, "as an antidote to any goldcraving influences which the story might arouse, the children could . . . read 'The Golden Touch,' by Hawthorne" (E. A. Poe, *The Gold-Bug*, ed. Theda Gildemeister [New York, 1902], p. 111).

3. Poe, review article, *Graham's* (November, 1841).

4. Numbers in the text refer to pages of "The Gold-Bug" in the *Collected Works of Edgar Allan Poe*, ed. Thomas Olive Mabbott (Cambridge, Mass., 1978), hereafter referred to as *CW*. Mabbott follows the text of the J. C. Lorimer Graham copy of *Tales*.

Washington Irving's "The Money-Diggers" is discussed by Robert J. Blanch, "The Background of Poe's 'Gold-Bug,' " *English Record*, 16 (1966), 44–45. Seba Smith's "The Money Diggers," which was published in *Burton's Magazine* (VII [August, 1840], pp. 81 ff.), is discussed by Killis Campbell, "Miscellaneous Notes on Poe," *MLN*, 28 (1913), 65–66.

5. See, for example, Carroll Laverty, "The Death's-Head on the Gold-Bug," *American Literature*, 12 (1940); and Ellison A. Smyth, Jr., "Poe's Gold Bug from the Standpoint of an Entomologist," *Sewanee Review*, 18 (1910), 67–72. Smyth argues that the bug in "The Gold-Bug" is one (or some combination of)the following: *Callichroma splendidum*, *Alaus oculatus*, *Phanoeus carnifex* (dung-beetle) and *Euphoria fulgida*.

6. *All in the Wrong* is the *wrong* source. Frederick Reynold's *The Dramatist* (1789) is more likely, but equally irrelevant.

7. Thomas Wyatt's *Synopsis of Natural History* (1839), esp. p. 128.

8. Mabbott's gloss for counters—"old coins, not current"—is unlikely. Counters were pieces used for calculation on a kind of abacus.

9. Baudelaire, p. 47. Baudelaire remarks that all of the coins were gold, but he forgets that before the chest itself was discovered the treasure-hunters found "three or four loose pieces of gold and silver coin" ("The Gold-Bug," p. 825). But perhaps Baudelaire was thinking only of the passage that concerns the treasure chest itself (pp. 827–28).

10. Smyth, pp. 71–72.

11. Marie Bonaparte, *The Life and Works of Edgar Allan Poe: A Psycho-Analytic Interpretation* (London, 1949), pp. 353–69, makes the conventional psychoanalytic argument. (Freud himself uses the term *Dukatenschiesser* in regard to another problem.) Bonaparte also draws attention to "the phallic significance of the golden insect" (p. 368), and notes that the "filth" here is to be interpreted also as "mother earth."

12. Barton Levi St. Armand, "Poe's 'Sober Mystification': The Uses of Alchemy in 'The Gold-Bug,' " *Poe Studies*, 4 (1971), 6.

13. *Literary World* (August 18, 1849), p. 133. Cf. Poe's "Diddling Considered as One of the Exact Sciences."

14. Mabbott, *CW*, 804.

15. "D," in *Philadelphia Daily Forum* (June 27, 1843). William Henry Gravely, Jr., who quotes the passage ("An Incipient Libel Suit Involving Poe," in *MLN*, 60 [1945],

309–10), claims that "D" was Francis H. Duffee. P's editorial appears in the *Public Ledger* (July 4, 1843), p. 2, col. 4.

16. Most tales are told with some reward in mind. The extreme example is Scheherazade who tells the tales of *The Thousand and One Nights* because she wants to live. "The Gold-Bug" earned Poe, the author of "The Thousand-and-Second Tale of Scheherazade," a partial livelihood out of a narrative interpretation of the symbol of death (the death's skull nailed in the branch), and was published in London as "No. 1" of a never-completed series entitled *The One Thousand and One Romances*. See Arthur Hobson Quinn, *Edgar Allan Poe: A Critical Biography* (New York, 1941), p. 392.

17. I distinguish between fiduciary money (bank notes) and scriptural money (created by the process of book-keeping). (Cf. Fernand Braudel, *Capitalism and Material Life: 1400–1800*, trans. Miriam Kochan [New York, 1975], pp. 357–72.) I also distinguish between the use of monies by small groups of people (scriptural money by merchants and bankers in eleventh-century Italy, for example) and its widespread use by the general population (fiduciary money by the French during the short-lived paper money experiment of John Law [1720], for example, and the almost continuous use of paper money by the Americans). On the early history of paper money in America (since before 1686), see Eric P. Newman, *The Early Paper Money of America* (Racine, Wisconsin, 1967).

18. Thomas Love Peacock, *Paper Money Lyrics* (1837), uses the term "paper money men." By "the end of the nineteenth century the term 'gold bug' was applied in America to scheming capitalists like Jay Gould [cf. Gold], who tried to corner the gold market, or to fanatical advocates of a gold standard over a silver standard" (St. Armand, p. 7, note 20).

19. Plates I and II are reproduced from David A. Wells, *Robinson Crusoe's Money; or the Remarkable Financial Fortunes and Misfortunes of a Remote Island Community* (New York, 1931).

20. In Goethe's *Faust*, for example, the banknote (*Geldschein*) as ghost (*Gespenst*) is a major *topos*, and in Karl Marx's works paper money is frequently associated with the shadow of Peter Schlemihl. See Marc Shell, "Money and the Mind: The Economics of Translation in Goethe's *Faust*," *MLN*, 94 (April, 1980).

21. Cf. the "ghastliness" of Legrand (p. 814).

22. *The Story of Canada's Currency*, second edition (Ottawa: Printed for the Royal Bank of Canada, 1966), p. 13.

23. See Ted N. Weissbuch, "A Note on the Confidence-Man's Counterfeit Detector," *Emerson Quarterly*, 19 (1960), 16–18; and William H. Dillistin, *Bank Note Reporters and Counterfeit Detectors* (New York, 1949) (*Numismatic Notes and Monographs*, No. 114 [Am. Num. Soc.]).

24. See Charles Feidelson, *Symbolism and American Literature* (Chicago, 1953), esp. p. 159.

25. Braudel, pp. 257–58.

26. "You send these notes out into the world stamped with irredeemability. You put on them the mark of Cain, and, like Cain, they will go forth to be vagabonds and fugitives on the earth . . . ." Representative George Pendleton (Ohio) thus opposed the issuance of legal tender in January 29, 1862 (*Congressional Globe*, 37th Congress, 2nd Sess. 1, 549 ff.; rpt. in P. A. Samuelson and H. E. Krooss, *Documentary History of Banking and Currency in the United States* [New York, Toronto, London, Sydney, 1969]).

27. Clinton Roosevelt, "On the Paradox of Political Economy in the Coexistence of Excessive Production and Excessive Population," in *Proceedings of the American Association for the Advancement of Science*, 13th Meeting, August, 1859 (Cambridge, 1860), pp. 344–52. See Joseph Dorfman, *The Economic Mind in American Civilization, 1606–1865* (New York, 1946), Vol. 2, 660–61.

On the Loco-Focos, see Arthur M. Schlesinger, *The Age of Jackson* (Boston, 1945), esp. pp. 198–99.

28. For relevant discussions see Marc Shell, "The Cancelled Bond: Dialectic and Monetary Form in Kant and Hegel," *Philosophy and Social Criticism*, 6 (Summer, 1979); and *The Economy of Literature* (Baltimore, 1978), esp. "Plato and the Money Form" in Chapter One. The "realists" adopted the line that only gold was substantial and the "idealists" (nominalists) took the part of the paper money men.

29. See Marchand, p. 40.

30. See Schlesinger, p. 232.

31. Allusions to the contemporary debate about gold and paper money include Poe's depiction of the man with the bandaged leg in "King Pest" (1835). This man recalls Colonel Thomas Hart Benton, a senator who led President Jackson's fight for gold (Benton was called "Old Bullion" and gold coins were called "Benton mint drops") and against paper money (or "shin plasters"). Cf. William Whipple, "Poe's Political Satire," *Texas Studies in English*, 35 (1956), 83, 86.

In the early 1840's Poe "enlisted the friendly aid of John Pendleton Kennedy" whose book, *Quodlibet*, was an allegorical attack on the institution of paper money (Marchand, p. 31). For an assessment of *Quodlibet*, see Vernon L. Parrington, *Main Currents in American Thought* (New York, 1954), vol. 2, 53–54: "*Quodlibet* is one of our few distinguished political satires."

32. In "Mellonta Tauta," Poe quotes Lucretius, *De rerum natura*: "Ex nihilo nihil fit." For the association of paper money with a nothing supposed to create all things, see the caricatures of John Law's paper money system and their accompanying inscriptions (described in *Catalogue of Prints and Drawings in the British Museum* [London, 1873], Division I: Political and Personal Satires, Volume II: June 1689 to 1733, esp. nos. 1610 to 1726).

33. St. Armand, p. 5.

34. Aristotle, *Politics* 1258.

35. In one sense paper money is and should be more valuable than specie. Thus Fernand Braudel (p. 365) notes that in Amsterdam as early as the eighteenth century "the 'ideal' bank money, the *florin de banque*, was quoted higher than real money in circulation, because of the inadequacies of circulating currency." In Hawthorne's "Seven Vagabonds," the beggar cashes the bill, but only at a discount unfavorable to the narrator.

36. Jupiter's reference to "bug mouff" recalls a third sound- and look-alike: the "moth" called "Death's Head Sphinx" which plays a role in Poe's "Sphinx" and was depicted in contemporary journals (e.g., *Saturday Magazine*, 25 August 1832). Elsewhere in Poe ("Some Words with a Mummy") the scarabeus is mentioned as the "insignium" of Egyptian families.

37. Legrand's penning the design of the new-found specimen of beetle has the apparent effect of introducing to the room a "Newfoundland" dog (p. 809). In the tale this dog plays a number of key roles. His "mouth/mouffe" (p. 823) and "claws/cause" (p. 825) recall those of the gold bug that bit Legrand with its mouth and so caused the bug for gold. And immediately upon the entrance of the Newfoundland dog, Legrand catches sight of a new-found design (the pirate's death's-head) that leads him to new-found treasure under the land.

The dog growls and scratches at the door much as does the poodle (Mephistopheles) before his first entrance in Goethe's *Faust*. As the dog's appearance accompanies Legrand's penning his design, so Mephistopheles' appearance accompanies Faust's penning his translation of Word into Act.

38. Legrand makes his bug hum when he swings it by the string (pp. 817, 844). (Cf. St. Armand and Bonaparte [p. 368] on the bee-line in "The Gold-Bug" and "The Black Cat.") This reaffirms the sense in which Legrand himself regards the bug as a hoax—a humbug—and the swinging of it as a bit of "mystification" (p. 847).

39. Poe writes that "the Romans worshipped their standards; and the Roman standard happened to be an eagle. Our standard is only one tenth of an Eagle—a dollar—but we make all even by adoring it with ten-fold devotion" ("Marginalia," in *Works*, ed. Harrison, vol. 16, 161.)

40. See W. K. Wimsatt, Jr., "What Poe Knew about Cryptography," *PMLA*, 58 (1943), 775–79; and J. Woodrow Hassell, Jr., "The Problem of Realism in 'The Gold-Bug,'" *American Literature*, 25 (1953), 179–92. For criticism involving other aspects of "verisimilitude" in the tale, see the discussion of the tulip-tree and its location in Eric Stockton, "Poe's Use of Negro Dialect in 'The Gold-Bug,'" *Studies in Languages and Linguistics in Honor of Charles C. Fries* (Ann Arbor, 1964), pp. 249–70; and Albert H. Tolman's "Was Poe Accurate?," *The Dial* (March 16, 1899), rpt. in Tolman, *The Views about Hamlet and Other Essays* (Boston and New York, 1904).

41. Newman, p. 93.

42. Ralph Waldo Emerson, "Nature," in *The Collected Works of Ralph Waldo Emerson*, ed. A .R. Ferguson (Cambridge, Mass., 1971), vol. 1, 20.

43. Umberto Eco argues that "the only difference between a coin (as sign-vehicle) and a word is that the word can be reproduced without economic effort while a coin is an irreproducible item (which shares some of the characters of its commondity-object)" (Eco, *A Theory of Semiotics* [Bloomington, 1979], p. 25; cf. F. Rossi-Landi, *Il linguagio come lavoro e come mercato* [Milan, 1968]). Eco relies on Karl Marx's analysis of the relationship between money and commodity. This is not the place to discuss whether Eco correctly interprets Marx's analysis of that relationship and whether Marx's analysis comprises an acceptable explanation of what a coin is. It is here significant, however, that Eco neglects to take into his general account of money and commodities the distinction between coins and paper money, a distinction that most monetary theorists (including Marx) consider.

44. "One might say: in all cases one means by thought what is living in the sentence. That without which it is dead, a mere sound sequence or sequence of written shapes . . . . Or what if we spoke of a something that distinguishes paper money from mere printed slips of paper and [that] gives [paper money] its meaning, its life." L. Wittgenstein, *Zettel*, ed. Anscombe and von Wright (Berkeley and Los Angeles, 1970), sect. 143.

45. For example: Marx, *Capital* (New York, 1967), vol. 1, 127; and Marx, *Critique of Political Economy* (New York, 1970), p. 116.

46. On Goolah, see Lorenzo Turner, *Africanisms in Gullah Dialect* (Chicago, 1949). The connection between gold and Goolah has to be stressed because critics have obscured it. Thus Stockton (p. 255) observes that Jupiter's "goole" (which occurs nine times in the tale) is merely "an interesting survival of the conservative pronunciation of 'gold' as /guld/." He neglects to consider the additional "e" that makes Jupiter's "goole" sound like "Goolah."

47. Ambrose Gonzales, *The Black Border: Gullah Stories of the Carolina Coast* (Columbia, S.C., 1922), esp. pp. 12–23.

48. Reading the story aloud makes the sound especially important. The dramatization of the tale in Silas S. Steele's *The Gold-Bug, or, The Pirate's Treasure* (1843) made it even more so. On the play, see Arthur A. Wilson, *History of the Philadelphia Theatre, 1835–1855* (Philadelphia, 1935).

49. *Southern Literary Messenger* (Richmond, Virginia, 1838), IV, 641/1.

50. *An* in Greek means "no" in English. Hence "antennae" might be understood as "no tin in him."

51. See, for example, Killis Campbell, *The Mind of Poe and Other Studies* (Cambridge, Mass., 1933), p. 113, n. 2, and p. 115.

52. In "The Gold-Bug" a parallel is made between aesthetic imagination, which seems able to transform a mere nothing into something, and "the agency of no human" (p. 831), of the devil. Satan—"sartain" (pp. 812, 820, 824)—confers the "debil's own lot of money" (p. 831).

53. In his translation of "The Gold-Bug"—"Le Scarabée d'Or"—Baudelaire translated "gose" as "oix" (goose). Mabbott (*CW*, 845–46) calls this an error, but "goose" is not incorrect.

The last major conversation in Melville's *Confidence Man* turns about a potential goose's attempt to match up the design of a goose in his Counterfeit Detector with the design of a goose on a banknote that he is attempting to authenticate. "Stay, now, here's another sign. It says that, if the bill is good, it must have in one corner . . . a goose . . . I can't see this goose" . . . "I don't see it—dear me—I don't see the goose. Is it a real goose?" The confidence man responds: "A perfect goose; beautiful goose" (Chapter LXV). On Melville's economics of symbolism, see Shell, *The Economy of Literature*, pp. 83–85.

54. N. P. Willis, *Tortesa the Usurer* (New York, 1839), Act 1, Scene 1. Poe writes that Willis's play is, "we think by far the best play from the pen of an American author" (*Burton's Gentleman's Magazine* [August 1839]).

55. Marc Shell, "The Wether and the Ewe: Verbal Usury in *The Merchant of Venice*," *The Kenyon Review*, N.S. 1 (Fall, 1979).

56. Heraclitus, frag. 22, in H. Diels, *Fragmente der Vorsokratiker*, 5th ed. (Berlin, 1934).

57. Cf. Levin, pp. 138–39.

58. While Poe has Legrand wander at a "beach" (p. 807) in the J. Lorimer copy of the last manuscript with revisions about 1849, the original version printed in *The Dollar Newspaper* of 1843 has Legrand conducting his search for conchological and etymological species at a "bank." Perhaps Poe wished to play down the explicitness of the financial theme in the new edition.

The Image in the Mirror: The Double Economy of James's *Portrait*

Edgar A. Dryden
University of Arizona

The "future of fiction," Henry James writes, "is intimately bound up with the future of the society that produces and consumes it."[1] The art of the novel, therefore, is one involving both aesthetics and economy, and the metaphors that James habitually uses to describe that art carry a heavy economic content. James recognizes that novels are merchandise, commodities produced to be exchanged for something else, and that at least part of the connection between writer and reader is a contract relation.[2] The fact that the novel has an exchange value establishes it as an economic as well as an aesthetic object and generates a tension that gives rise to problems of intention and meaning. Are its words used in a "moral or financial sense"?[3] Is the novelist motivated by the "sublime economy of art"[4] or by the crass desire to "put money in [his] pocket" (*PL*, p. 431)? And is the reader an appreciator or consumer? Does he devour the book driven only by the appetite for story or does he read carefully and slowly with an eye to effect and style? The problem of figurative language, the question of representation, the issue of the relation between writer and reader: these are the recurring concerns of James's Prefaces, and his discussion of them is informed by language of domestic and political economy. This is especially true of the Preface to *The Portrait of a Lady*, for that is a novel directly concerned with the relation between the aesthetic and the economic, between works of art and money.

The Preface focuses on a double problem: the nature of the writer's relation to his art and the form of his relationship to his reader, that is to say on the problem of representing and reading. I intend here to explore some aspects of this double problem as it appears in the Preface and the novel by investigating the dual economies that govern it. One can begin by noticing that the figure of the reader haunts the Preface to the *Portrait*, infusing its ghostly presence into the essay's metaphoric details and interrupting and delaying James's attempt to recover the "germ" of his idea for the novel. This spectre is the representative of an exterior realm, a world outside the writer's sanctuary, and he threatens to compromise the writer's artistic ideals and to violate his solitude.

The essay begins, appropriately, with the figure of the novelist at the window of his Venice apartment "driven in the fruitless fidget of composition" (p. 3) to seek inspiration in the "sight of a wondrous lagoon" (p. 3). However, his appeal to that "romantic and historic" site fails, and that failure is expressed in figures that question the dignity and value of the act of writing.

> They are too rich in their own life and too charged with their own meanings merely to help him out with a lame phrase . . . so that, after a little, he feels while thus yearning toward them in his difficulty, as if he were asking any army of glorious veterans to help him arrest a pedlar who has given him the wrong change. (pp. 3–4)

The writer's search for "some better phrase," some "true touch for his canvas" (p. 3) is associated with the acts of haggling and cheating, and this chain of association is lengthened as James goes on to discuss the effect of beautiful places on the writer's imagination in terms of attention's being "wasted," "squandered," and "cheated" (p. 4). The act of writing from its beginning seems to depend on but to be contaminated by a world outside the walls of the writer's study. The relation between these exterior and interior spaces is expressed by a set of commercial metaphors that imply a series of exchanges destined to frustrate the writer's dreams of creating a self-sufficient and autonomous world.

Nevertheless, as James goes on to insist, the writer's "subject" appears to him pure and alone, free of the "tangle, to which we look for much of the impress that constitutes an identity" (p. 8), a vivid individual yet one independent of the "cluster of appurtenances" (p. 172) that normally represent the self. But if the writer's subject comes to him free of social tangles, it does not completely liberate him from a world of exchange. However, the subject does appear to make his relationship to that exterior world marginal and eccentric.

> The figure has to that extent, as you see, *been* placed—placed in the imagination that detains it, preserves, protects, enjoys it, conscious of his presence in the dusky, crowded, heterogeneous backstop of the mind very much as a wary dealer in precious odds and ends, competent to make an "advance" on rare

objects confided to him, is conscious of a rare little "piece" left in deposit by the reduced, mysterious lady of title or the speculative amateur, and which is already there to disclose its merit afresh as soon as a key shall have clicked in a cupboard-door.

That may be, I recognize, a somewhat superfine analogy for the particular "value" I here speak of . . . but it appears to fond memory quite to fit the fact—with the recall, in addition, of my pious desire but to place my treasure right. I quite remind myself thus of the dealer resigned not to "realize," resigned to keeping the precious object locked up indefinitely rather than commit it, at no matter what price, to vulgar hands. For there *are* dealers in these forms and figures and treasures capable of that refinement. (p. 8)

Although James carefully conceals the circumstances of his actual acquisition of the image of Isabel Archer, this elaborate figurative description of his relation to it suggests a host of complicating factors. The image is not yet surrounded by the "envelope of circumstances" (p. 172) that constitute society. Instead it remains at home within the writer's imagination that, like Mr. Venus' shop in *Our Mutual Friend*, is a dusky, crowded place filled with heterogeneous objects. There it retains its independence, for its relations to its surroundings is that of one discrete and unique object among others. Still the "value" of the "treasure" remains an entirely subjective one until it is placed within the "tangle of human relationships" (p. 63), and to place it means to remove it from the protective confines of the imagination and commit it to a realm where its value and meaning will be determined relationally. Moreover, since the act of placing the "treasure" is one of social and commerical engagement, the writer must leave the protective solitude of his eccentricity and enter a more conventional world.

To begin to write is to organize an "ado" for the "novel is by its very nature an ado about something" (p. 9).[5] Isabel, however, will remain central with the "ado" taking the form of "satellites" (p. 11). This strategy, James hopes, will resolve the conflict between his representational ideal—the proper placing of his "treasure"—and the necessity of piling "brick upon brick for the creation of an interest" (p. 11), between the "fine embossed vaults and painted arches" and the "chequered pavement" that forms the "ground under the reader's feet" (p. 11). The "ado" is provided by the characters who surround Isabel, characters who are to function as the "rockets, the Roman candles and Catherine-wheels of a 'pyrotechnic display'" (p. 11) and who are "like the group of attendants and entertainers who come down by train when people in the country give a party; they [represent] the contract for carrying the party on" (p. 12). No longer can the author envision himself as an eccentric pawnbroker, a dealer in precious odds and ends who relates only to mysterious aristocrats and speculative amateurs. These other metaphors suggest, rather, the professional entertainer and party giver; and, indeed, James emphasizes his "anxiety" regarding his provision for the reader's amusement, the "special obligation" that he feels "to be amusing" (p. 15). These figures suggest a form of exchange that differs in significant ways from those engaged in by the "wary dealer in precious odds and ends." In this case there is no question of protecting precious objects or of avoiding vulgar hands. And the only "benefit" that he can expect from his reader is a form of enchantment that is the result of a spell cast "upon the simpler, the very simplest form of attention." The "quantity of attention" that is required for consciousness of a spell is the "living wage" for which the novelist works and any act of "reflexion" or "discrimination" on the reader's part must be regarded a "tip" or "gratuity" (p. 12) thrown in. Any dreams of appealing directly to the reader's intelligence are extravagances that cannot be afforded. No longer is the novelist privileged as the owner of money always is over the owner of commodities. The balance of power has shifted. Now it is the novelist who has the commodity and his reader the money for which the commodity is to be exchanged, with the result that the novelist is in the inferior position both economically and socially. As Georg Simmel has noticed, the principle of supplement whereby the buyer demands and receives an extra measure points to the superior position of the owner of money. It is of course precisely the effort to provide that extra measure of amusement that causes James, as he says, to "overtreat" in his portrayal of Henrietta Stackpole. Moreover, as Simmel further notes, when the supplement is provided by the owner of money, as in the case of the gratuity, it simply expresses the social superiority of the giver.[6]

The Preface to *The Portrait of a Lady*, then, develops in the context of a chain of economic metaphors that presents a vision of the "artist doubled with a man of business" and this "monstrous duality"[7] generates two incompatible theories of artistic creation, the one associated with the pure vision of the artist, the other with the uncontrolled "appetite" of an "unreflective and uncritical"[8] reader. This is a conflict that is thematized within the novel itself, which like *Our Mutual Friend* is about "money, money, money and what money can make of life." Both Dickens and James are interested in the problems resulting from the inheritance of a great fortune and in the effects that the presence or absence of money has on human lives. For almost all of the characters in the *Portrait* the "money question [is] always a trouble" (*PL*, p. 368). The lack of money has narrowed severely the expectations of Osmond, Madame Merle, and the Countess Gemini and threatens the happiness of Rosier and Pansy. Indeed the world of the *Portrait* is one where the relations of people to one another, to social institutions, and to works of art are marked by monetary interests. As the expression and equivalent of all values money becomes the center of the novel's action, the secular god of its world.[9]

Ralph Touchet, fascinated by the figure of his attractive cousin, decides to make her independent in a "financial" as well as in a "moral" (*PL*, p. 24) sense in order that she be able to "meet the requirements of [her] imagination" (p. 158), but in so doing becomes the "beneficent author of infinite woe" (p. 351), for he makes her free to fall and thus condemns her to a life of "darkness and suffocation" (p. 355). This figurative pattern is elaborated by a set of Miltonic allusions that provide an ironic context for the development of Isabel's story. Feeling her new freedom, the "boldness and wantonness of liberty" (p. 267), Isabel bids farewell to her visiting American relations and prepares to begin her career.

> The world lay before her—she could do whatever she chose. There was a deep thrill in it all, but for the present her choice was tolerably discreet; she chose simply to walk back from Euston Square to her hotel. The early dusk of a November afternoon had already closed in . . . our heroine was unattended and Euston Square was a long way from Piccadilly. But Isabel performed the journey with a positive enjoyment of its dangers and lost her way almost on purpose, in order to get more sensations, so she was disappointed when an obliging policeman easily set her right again. (p. 267)

One effect of this allusion to *Paradise Lost* is to emphasize the reduction and impoverishment of the Christian myth which has become completely socialized and trivialized. Here Isabel appears most obviously as that "frail vessel" of which James writes in the Preface, one of the "smaller female fry" (p. 9) whose adventures can hardly be seen as possessing epic dignity. Nevertheless, James also insists that that "frail vessel" possesses the "high attributes of a subject" (p. 3) more in keeping with the Miltonic model. And in extravagantly elevating one of the "smaller female fry" to the status of the subject (a "task unattempted" [p. 9] by Scott, Dickens, and Stevenson) James himself assumes a Miltonic dignity. Once again, however, the central issue is the extent to which this artistic ideal is undermined by the demands of his story. And indeed James's description of Isabel as a "rare little piece" calls attention to a set of similar figures within the novel itself that copy and hollow out the one in the Preface. Its world is filled with "such valuable pieces" that are bought, sold, collected and admired for a variety of reasons. Isabel, alone in the gallery at Gardencourt near the end of the novel, offers a suggestive reading of the significance of such objects.

> She envied the security of valuable "pieces" which change by no hair's breadth, only grow in value, while their owners lose inch by inch youth, happiness, beauty; and she became aware that she was walking about as her aunt had done on the day she had come to see her in Albany. She was changed enough since then—that had been the beginning. (p. 464)

At issue here, of course, is a question of value, a word that appears repeatedly in the *Portrait* in a variety of contexts but almost always in a mode that entangles the ideas of aesthetic value and economic value. For example, the value of a "real collector's piece" (p. 296) is a double one: it possesses qualities that give it an inherent worth and that grant a certain dignity and authority to its owner; but it also enjoys an economic value that has little or nothing to do with its inherent qualities but that is established by the expenditure of another object in exchange for it. Economic objects have meaning only in terms of exchange. Appropriately, money, the medium of exchange, possesses no content of its own.[10] In the above passage these two very different notions of value are mixed and confused. The pieces are valuable, first, because like Keats's Urn they belong to an immutable world of art that is "All breathing human passion far above." Their beauty remains while that of their owners tragically fades. Nevertheless, in their changelessness they grow in value, for while their beauty and meaning remain the same, their exchange value increases. Hence Isabel is led to see herself in ironic relationship to them, for her economic value has grown too—thanks to Ralph's artistic interest in her fate—but at the expense of her innocence and happiness.

Isabel's meditation on these "valuable pieces" echoes not only James's description of her in the Preface as a "rare little piece" but also Ralph's appreciative reaction to her as "an interesting little figure" (p. 62). For her ill and bored cousin, she is "entertainment of a high order . . . finer than the finest work of art—than a Greek bas-relief, than a great Titian, than a Gothic cathedral" (p. 63). In a sense, Ralph's decision to "put money in her purse" (p. 158) is an attempt to make Isabel's economic value equal to her aesthetic value for it is designed to "facilitate the execution of good impulses" (p. 160). The effect, however, is to cause her "ruin" (p. 470) for it results in her becoming one of Gilbert Osmond's "fine pieces" (p. 302).

Osmond, of course, is another collector of "pictures . . . medallions and tapestries" (p. 219), a " few good things" that "hint that nothing but the right 'values' was of any consequence" (p. 215). Initially, Osmond sees Isabel as a "present of incalculable value," a fine object that will reflect his thought "on a polished elegant surface" (p. 290). Her value for him is that of a representation but in a social rather than an aesthetic sense. Like his other "treasures" she is esteemed because she will "extract" from the "base ignoble world . . . some suggestion of [Osmond's] own superiority" (p. 353). On the one hand he wants to disassociate himself from the vulgar world of commerce, to insist that he has never "scrambled or struggled" (p. 88) for money, that his interest in others is only for "their advantage, not for any profit to a person already so generally, so perfectly provided as Gilbert Osmond" (p. 391). On the other hand, however, his social relations are valued entirely for the "prospect of gain" (p. 391) that they promise.

This aspect of Osmond is rendered brilliantly by James both in his description of him as a "fine gold coin" but with "no stamp nor emblem of the common mintage that provides for general circulation; he was the elegant complicated medal struck off for a special occasion" (p. 144) and by the picture of him alone in his study meticulously copying from a book the "drawing of an antique coin" and transferring the "delicate, finely-tinted disk" to a "sheet of immaculate paper" (p. 436). Here at once is an indication of Osmond's "exquisite" taste and a sign that that "taste" (p. 286) has commercial origins. Osmond's "box of water colours and fine brushes" (p. 436), his immaculate paper, and the delicate disk cannot conceal the fact that he is reproducing a copy of a copy of an object that may itself have been mechanically reproduced, and that object is a token of money. Isabel's sense of her husband's "blasphemous sophistry" (p. 439) seems exactly to the point since both Plato and Aristotle associate the sophist with the exchange of apparent wisdom for money. Like the sophist Osmond insists that "what I value most in life is the honour of a thing" (p. 438) while demonstrating through his words and actions that like the monetary token whose image he copies his values are the product of an external impress.[11] All other objects have a content from which they derive value, but money derives its content from its value—it represents the values of things without the things themselves. Osmond's words are like coins because while they seem to represent "something transcendental and absolute, like the sign of the cross or the flag of one's country" (p. 439), they are in fact forms without a content.

In contrast to Osmond is Edward Rosier, another collector of "pretty things" (p. 299) who, with his "eye for decorative character, his instinct for authenticity," and a "sense of uncatalogued values" (p. 303) is capable of appreciating others in a way that Osmond is not. His interest in Pansy echoes with a difference Osmond's attraction to Isabel. Initially she seems to him a "consummate piece"—"He thought of her in amorous meditation a good deal as he would have thought of a Dresden-china shepherdess" (p. 296). But Rosier's attitude toward his things—"I love my things"—and toward Pansy—" 'I care more for Miss Osmond than for all the *bibelots* in Europe' " (p. 396)—indicates a sense of relation that Osmond never experiences. Osmond cares only for "one's money" (p. 310), and Rosier's "forty thousand francs a year and a nice character" (p. 299) fail to qualify him as a son-in-law. Recognizing that in Osmond's eyes he is not a "real collector's piece" (p. 296), Rosier exchanges his beloved *bibelots* for money: " 'I have the money instead—fifty thousand dollars' " (p. 431). Although he is careful to " 'put them into good hands,' " he gives them up in order to " 'put money in [his] pocket' " (p. 431). His interest, however, is not in money but in Pansy whom he loves. Earlier he had insisted that he can " 'buy very well, but . . . can't sell' " since it takes " 'much more ability to make other people buy than to buy yourself' " (p. 184), but now his love for Pansy introduces another and higher system of value that redirects and changes the meaning of his commercial transactions.

Isabel's relation to Ralph, Osmond, and Rosier—all of whom are collectors of interesting figures—develops in the context that echoes suggestively James's re-reading of the novel in the Preface. This echoing effect serves not only to contaminate the purity of his aesthetic ideal by associating him with the desires and limitations of his characters but also to confuse the ontological status of the characters thereby breaking the spell of art and disenchanting the reader. Once we see that the "figure" of Isabel is transferred from hand to hand—from an unknown source to James, to Ralph, to Osmond—we are caught in a sliding process that is impossible to stop at any one particular point or meaning. The characters like the author become for us irreducibly double, at once "authentic and elusive [people] moving through visible and tangible territories"[12] and painted portraits, valuable pieces in a tasteful collection of good things. And this sense of doubleness is present too in the theory of representation that governs the logic of both the Preface and novel and shapes the complex relation between James and his reader.

"The most fundamental and general sign of the novel" James writes in "The Lesson of Balzac," "is its being everywhere an effort at *representation*."[13] Indeed, the "only reason for the existence of a novel is that it does attempt to represent life."[14] However, as James recognizes, "people differ infinitely as to what . . . constitutes representation"[15] for the concept is more problematic than it first appears. James's model, of course, for his idea of representation is that of the painted image. For him the "analogy between the art of the painter and the art of the novelist is . . . complete."[16] A "community of method" exists between the "artist who paints a picture and the artist who writes the novel"; hence the novel can best be thought of as a "prose picture."[17]

This analogy between the painting and the novel informs James's literary and critical vocabulary and seems to provide a familiar and comfortable foundation for creative and interpretive activities, for it suggests not only a clear and unambiguous relation between the image and the represented entity, but a perfect compatibility between language and vision as well. For James, however, representation is a more problematic process than the analogy between painting and writing at first suggests. For him the process involves more than the mere duplication of sense data and hence cannot be thought of simply as imitation: "but the affair of the painter is not the immediate, it is the reflected field of life, the realm not of application, but of *appreciation*. . . . My report of people's experience—my report as a 'storyteller'—is essentially my appreciation of it. . . ."[18] Representation, in other words, is a constructive, interpretive act that derives from an "impression of life,"[19] life seen as an image, in a glass darkly, not face to face. The novelist does not depict the real but a represented or interpreted version of the real. Consequently, the art of the novel, unlike that of lyrical poetry, is not one of immediacy and presence.

> The Poet is most the Poet when he is preponderantly lyrical, when he speaks . . . most directly from his individual heart, which throbs under the impressions of life. It is not the *image* of life that he thus expresses, as much as life itself, in its sources—so much as his own intimate, essential states and feelings. By the time he has begun to collect anecdotes, to tell stories, to represent scenes, to concern himself, that is, with states and feelings of others, he is well on the way not to be the poet pure and simple.[20]

As "lovers of the image of life" novelists seem to prefer distance and difference to a sense of unmediated presence. The novel is precisely a "monument,"[21] a "bequest"[22] that is, the record of an absence, a deferred and indirect account of a direct exposure. "There is, to my vision, no authentic, and no really interesting and no *beautiful*, report of things on the novelist's, the painter's part unless a particular detachment has operated, unless . . . the observant and recording and interpreting mind in short has intervened and played its part—and this detachment, this chemical transmutation for the aesthetic, the representational end is wanting in autobiography brought, as the horrible phrase is, up to date."[23]

James's view of representation, then, complicates that of the one traditionally associated with realism. For him the novel is not simply the verbal representation of social reality, a "standing for" or a "standing in place of" something that exists somewhere else and in another time. Prior to the act of verbally representing is the "power of life to project itself upon [man's] imagination" and to produce the "impressions" that are "experience," the "very air we breath."[24] And since "experience" for James is "our apprehension of what happens to us as social creatures,"[25] the source of that "power" is the figure of the other. Consequently, the act of literary representation is subsequent to and depends on another form of representation, one that comes into play whenever the self confronts the other.[26]

Selves, for James, are not accessible to one another in direct or obvious ways. His novels insist on the importance of "feel[ing] one's relation . . . to others" (*PL*, p. 286) and at the same time emphasize the distance and difference that disturb and problematicize any attempt to establish meaningful relations to others. His characters come to see that selfhood depends on the presence of others and yet that presence is experienced as a kind of absence. Others appear to me—they are there—but they appear as aliens; they present themselves as unpresentable. They cannot, in other words, be present to me in their own persons, and hence some form of representation is called for.[27] To represent the self is to offer something to stand in its place, something that is not the self but that is, perhaps, analogous to it. For this reason the self always appears as a sign, an image necessitating reading, appreciation, interpretation. Hence the concept of identity itself is a form of representation to the extent that it is a social category and is defined in terms of "career . . . name . . . position . . . fortune . . . past . . . future" (*PL*, p. 169). For Madame Merle, Ralph

Touchet's selfhood is represented by his consumption, which is a "kind of position." His father, on the other hand, "represents a great financial house" (p. 169), while Gilbert Osmond may only be defined in terms of his painting and the fact that he is a father. Nor is this attitude simply an expression of Madame Merle's cynicism, for most of the characters in *The Portrait of a Lady* exist in such a representational mode. Henrietta Stackpole is the "representative of the *Interviewer*" (p. 175); Lord Warburton, "a fine specimen," is a "representative of the British race" (p. 242); Isabel represents Gilbert Osmond and Pansy "represents" Isabel's "responsibility" (p. 292).

As Laurence Holland has noticed, this form of representation differs in obvious ways from the model of representational painting that is suggested by the title of the *Portrait* and by the association of sketching and writing within the novel.[28] The nature of the relationship that exists between the two models is suggested by Lord Warburton's assertion that " 'You can't see ideas' " (*PL*, p. 23). Like feeling and emotions ideas belong to inward experience and depend on some form of representation to make them visible. The more complicated the idea, of course, the more difficult the problem of representing it becomes. " 'The two words in the language' " Mrs. Touchet " 'most respects are Yes and No' " (p. 230), presumably because the distance between the word and the idea it represents is bridgeable and remains stable. However, the inner world of James and those of most of his characters are too complicated to be represented so simply. Ralph's vision of things, for example, requires such a "fanciful, pictorial way of saying things" that Mrs. Touchet feels that she is being addressed in a "deaf mute's alphabet" (p. 230). " 'I don't know what you mean' she said, 'You use too many figures of speech: I never could understand allegories' " (p. 230).

James, of course, shares Mrs. Touchet's dislike of allegory, a process he describes as a "story told as if it were another and very different story."[29] Nevertheless, as he recognizes, metaphor has its allegorical aspects in the sense that it is an attempt to represent in words that which we experience, and experience for James consists of impressions, of seeing. Hence his ideal of the "prose picture" expresses a desire to be able to say what he sees, to render exactly the image that appears in the mirror. However, as the example of Ralph and his mother makes clear, the realms of vision and language are not equivalents. What is seen, of course, is itself a sign, and Ralph's highly metaphoric language problematicizes rather than clarifies the lines between the human hieroglyph and its verbal signifier by making the primary question one of the nature between the figures themselves. What, for example, does a "tender young rose" (p. 189) have in common with a bird, an encastled princess, a physician, a steam ship or a sailing vessel, all of which are figures that Ralph uses to describe Isabel?

Ralph's problem in describing his vision of Isabel is mirrored by that of his creator. James's description of Isabel's vigil as the "best thing in the book" and a "supreme illustration of the book's general plan" points directly to the problem, for the chapter is a "representation simply of her motionless seeing" (p. 14), a moment of pure vision, yet it possesses too the interest of the sequential aspects of narrative. Few critics would quarrel with James's aesthetic assessment of this admirable chapter. Nevertheless, in some ways, it, like Ralph's pictorial way of speaking, points to the incompatibility between language and vision. To be sure the chapter is in an important sense the "portrait of a lady," but it is also a revelation of the differences that exist between words and pictures, since it demonstrates that neither can be completely reduced to the other's terms.

It is true that Isabel, motionless and alone, seems to occupy a space where she is free only to look, but it is equally true that that space is filled both for her and the reader by signs of an intrusive temporality. Her vision is of a tangle of relationships that are represented by her departed husband's words. "She had answered nothing because his words had put the situation before her and she was absorbed in looking at it. There was something in them that suddenly made vibrations deep, so that she had been afraid to trust herself to speak. After he had gone she leaned back in her chair and closed her eyes; and for a long time, far into the night and still further, she sat in the still drawing room given up to her meditation" (p. 347). Osmond's words seem at first to have been transformed into a picture thereby placing Isabel's situation within the space of her vision. This moment of insight, however, has been generated partially by the "strange impression that she had received in the afternoon of her husband's being in more direct communication with Madame Merle than she suspected" (p. 349), and hence does not occur in the form of an unambiguous flash of meaning; rather, it manifests itself as a series of readings or interpretations that take the form of successive moments in a narrative. Isabel must "read" (p. 348) the signs of Warburton's attitude in order to grasp the relation between his past desires and present intentions; place those interpretations within the context of her knowledge that her problems with Osmond derive from the fact that "she had not read him right" (p. 351) as well as her sense that she can now "read" him "as she would have read the hour on the clock-face" (p. 356); and, finally, decide how her current reading of Osmond is to shape her relations to Warburton, Ralph and Pansy.

Isabel's vision, then, is both the result and expression of an uninterrupted and irresistible flow of time, and James's portrayal of that "motionless seeing" reveals time's erosive power. Movement persists in spite of the illusion of simultaneity for the moment of insight is spread out across a temporal field marked by Warburton's arrival at 10:00 p.m., his departure half an hour later, Osmond's appearance at eleven, and the clock's striking four at the end of the chapter.

The tension in this chapter between the spatial and the temporal, between what James calls the "economy of picture" and the "economy of interest,"[30] is a thematization of the relation between the acts of writing and reading as James understands them. Hence the chapter is illustrative in yet another sense since it represents in a synecdochic fashion a central problem of the novel. The painterly model which James emphasizes in the title of *The Portrait of a Lady* and develops within the novel is partially subverted by a paradigm of textuality. Against the notion of the novel as a "sketch" or "prose picture" and against the ideal of moments of pure vision James sets the suggestion that both characters and novelist are readers of a text caught within a system of signs that, like one of Mrs. Touchet's puzzling telegrams, "admit of so many interpretations" (*PL*, p. 24). Isabel seems to her brother-in-law to be "written in a foreign tongue. I can't make her out" (p. 37). Warburton must be "read" by Isabel "more or less between the lines" (p. 390), while Ralph in his dealings with Henrietta Stackpole, who "challenged all his ingenuity of interpretation," finds it easier "to read between the lines . . . than to follow the text" (p. 109). Pansy, in her innocence, is like a "blank sheet of paper," a "fair and smooth page" (p. 233) that Isabel hopes will "be covered with an edifying text" (p. 262), while the well used Countess Gemini "has been written over in a variety of hands" and has a "number of unmistakable blots . . . upon her surface" (p. 233).

If the interpersonal world of social relations may be thought of as a text, Mr. Touchet's assertion that he receives "information in the natural form" (p. 57) rather than through books is put into question as is, in a different way, Isabel's dream of being free and open to pure experience. Although she has a bookish reputation and is found by her aunt "reading a heavy book and boring herself to death" (p. 47) Isabel, like her uncle, "really preferred almost any source of information to the printed page," hence her eyes characteristically "wander from the book in her hand to the open window" (p. 475). Books for Isabel are little more than distractions, and while she holds them and fingers them, she seldom reads them. We see her holding a book but "without going through the form of opening the volume" (p. 143), find her "seated in a library with a volume to which her attention was not fastened" (p. 176) or "holding a volume of Ampere . . . in her lap with her finger vaguely kept in the place" (p. 255). Indeed, in the world of *The Portrait of a Lady* books, like those "rare and valuable volumes" (p. 475) in Ralph's library, are objects to be held, their pages fingered, their bindings admired and then to be set carefully aside. Like Madame Merle's "pastimes," books are "laid down" (p. 165) as easily as taken up and reading as an activity is neither more nor less valuable than letter writing, painting, "touching the piano," or any other "cultivated and cultured" (p. 164) activity.

As the textuality paradigm suggests, however, these bound volumes are parts of a larger socially given text, and it is this larger text that draws Isabel's attention from the specifically literary ones.

> Seated toward nine o'clock in the dim illumination of Pratt's Hotel and trying with the aid of two tall candles to lose herself in a volume she had brought from Gardencourt, she succeeded only to the extent of reading other words than those printed on the page—words that Ralph had spoken to her that afternoon. Suddenly the well-muffled knuckle of the waiter was applied to the door, which presently gave way to his exhibition, even as a glorious trophy, of the card of a visitor. When this momento had offered to her fixed sight the name of Mr. Casper Goodwood she let the man stand before her without signifying her wishes.
>
> "Shall I show the gentleman up, ma'am?" he asked with a slightly encouraging inflexion.
>
> Isabel hesitated still and while she hesitated glanced at the mirror. "He may come in," she said at last; and waited for him not so much smoothing her hair as girding her spirit. (p. 134)

Spoken discourse no less than the written text must be read. Like calling cards, those "oblong morsels of symbolic pasteboard" (p. 59), or like one's image in the mirror, spoken words as a form of representation imply that the subject is not present in his own person. As Isabel seeks to "lose herself" in the book she is confronted first by the image of Ralph's vision of her future—the "world interests you and you want to throw yourself into it" (p. 132)—then by the calling card, a sign that stands for another person and yet another version of her destiny, and finally, by her own mirror image, a two dimensional reflection of her body on glass that manages nevertheless to represent her ambivalent relation to Goodwood, the extent to which she wishes both to attract and resist him. Following their conversation and Goodwood's departure Isabel once again "takes up her book, but without going through the form of opening the volume" (p. 143), and enjoys the memory of what she takes to be the first "exercise of her power," the expression of her "love of liberty," only to be reminded by Henrietta that her ideas of happiness resemble those of the heroine of an "immoral novel" (p. 144).

This episode is an interesting one because it opens up the problem of the book, setting experience and natural information against secondary book knowledge but also putting such a formulation into question by revealing the textual nature of the world of ordinary discourse. This, of course, is an important issue for James as well as for Isabel as the emphasis on reading in the Preface makes clear. Like Isabel James at times seems to privilege direct experience over written accounts of it: "One can read when one is middle-aged or old," he writes to his brother, William, "but one can mingle in the world with fresh perceptions only when one is young. The great thing is to be *saturated* with something, that is, in one way or another with life; and I choose the form of my saturation. Moreover, you exaggerate the degree to which my writing takes it out of my mind, for I try to spend only the interest of my capital."[31] This interesting comment parallels Isabel's attitude and situation in a variety of ways. James too insists that he "wants to see for myself" (*PL*, p. 132), to experience direct impressions rather than to secure them secondhand by the way of books. However, his primary concern is not his liberty or personal independence but the act of writing, for it depends upon his being saturated with life. Unlike reading, writing seems to be directly concerned with life and to depend on a direct involvement with it. In that sense it is productive, active economic activity that refines and improves life.

> Life being all inclusion and confusion, and art being all discrimination and selection, the latter, in search of the hard latent *value* with which alone it is concerned, sniffs round the mass as instinctively and unerringly as a dog suspicious of some buried bone. The difference here, however, is that, while the dog desires his bone but to destroy it, the artist finds in his tiny *nugget*, washed free of awkward accretions and hammered into a sacred hardness, the

very stuff for a clear affirmation, the happiest chance for the indestructible. It at the same time amuses him again and again to note how, beyond the first step of the actual case, the case that constitutes for him his germ, his vital particle, his grain of gold, life persistently blunders and deviates, loses herself in the sand. The reason is of course that life has no direct sense whatever for the subject and is capable, luckily for us, of nothing but splendid waste. Hence the opportunity for the sublime economy of art, which rescues, which saves, and hoards and "banks," investing and reinvesting these fruits of toil in wondrous useful "works" and thus making up for us, desperate spendthrifts that we all naturally are, the most princely of incomes.[32]

This suggestive passage nicely illuminates the complexities of James's double economy. It begins with what seems to be a clear explanation of the special value of the "prose picture" that is based on an unambiguous distinction between the realms of art and life. Like the textuality paradigm, however, the economic metaphor contaminates the ideal of pure vision by way of notions of equivalence and exchange. As a product, this passage implies, the novel must submit itself to an economic system and become merchandise subject to desires other than those that produced it. Unlike the writer, the reader is often concerned with the "fact of consumption"[33] and regards the novel as a "good dinner" with a happy ending being a "course of dessert and ices and the artist in the fiction . . . as a sort of meddlesome doctor who forbids agreeable aftertastes."[34] This is the reader who will "consume" fiction "on the scale and with the smack of lips that mark the consumption of bread-and-jam by a children's school-feast."[35] It is perhaps this aspect of the reading process that leads James to write that "I am a wretched person to *read* a novel—I begin so quickly and concomitantly, *for myself*, to write it rather—even before I know clearly what it's about! The novel I can *only* read, I can't read at all!"[36]

Nevertheless writing and reading are inextricably entangled, the one act inevitably conditioned by, dependent on the other. In this sense the art of the novelist like that of the physician is the result of the flawed human condition. From the reader's point of view the novel is an "anodyne" that like the "dentist's ether, muffles the ache of the actual"[37] by offering us another world (p. 321). It is that "ache" that is responsible for man's "appetite for picture," a vicarious desire for the derived and secondhand.

And if we are pushed a step farther backward, and asked why the representation should be required when the object represented is itself mostly so accessible, the answer to that appears to be that man combines with his eternal desire for more experience an infinite cunning as to getting his experience as cheaply as possible. He will steal it whenever he can. He likes to live the life of others, yet is well aware of the points at which it may too intolerably resemble his own. The vivid fable, more than anything else, gives him this satisfaction on easy terms, gives him knowledge abundant yet vicarious. It enables him to select, to take and to leave; so that to feel he can afford to neglect it, he must have a rare faculty, or great opportunities for the extension of experience . . . at first hand.[38]

Because fiction creates the illusion that "for a time . . . we have lived another life," it allows us to "live at the expense of someone else,"[39] to satisfy our desire for experience but to avoid being "exposed and entangled"[40] ourselves. Now the principles of economy and representation operating here differ in obvious and important ways from the "sublime economy of art" and the notion of the prose picture that James usually associates with the act of writing. Writing as an activity is usually linked to saving, investing and reinvesting, to the production of the "most princely of incomes." Reading, on the other hand, is an activity engaged in by someone too poor or too lazy to approach experience directly and is associated with a low-class commercial world of haggling and cheating. Moreover the overwhelming "appetite for picture" establishes a "demand" that threatens the "splendid . . . economy" of the novel[41] by causing it to become an "object of easy manufacture," an "article of commerce." The result is a flood of "monstrous multiplications" and the "bankrupt state"[42] of the novel as a form.

The acts of reading and writing, then, appear, paradoxically, to be mutually dependent but incompatible activities. The "object" of the novel is to represent life but the "effect" is to "entertain,"[43] and the "effect" seems to contaminate the "object." *The Portrait of a Lady* represents James's attempt to harmonize these two opposing principles. However, the artist is governed by one economic law and the reader has another, so that the two economies can never be congruous. The principle of composition is always dislocated by the principle of consumption, the act of writing in perpetual conflict with the act of reading. It is this incompatibility that becomes for James the very mark of the novel as a form, at once the sign of its flawed nature and the source of its enormous energy. As he says in "The Future of the Novel," man will renounce fiction "only when life itself too thoroughly disagrees with him. Even then, indeed, may fiction not find a second wind, or a fiftieth, in the very portrayal of that collapse. Till the world is an unpeopled void there will be an image in the mirror."[44]

NOTES

1. Henry James, "The Future of the Novel," in *Henry James: Selected Literary Criticism*, ed. Morris Shapira (London: Heinemann, 1963), p. 185.
2. For a suggestive discussion of this issue see Roland Barthes, *S/Z*, trans. Richard Miller (New York: Hill and Wang, 1974), pp. 88–92.
3. Henry James, *The Portrait of a Lady*, ed. Leon Edel (Boston: Houghton Mifflin, 1963), p. 24. All further references to the *Portrait* and to its Preface will be to this edition, and the novel will be indicated in the text by the abbreviation *PL*.
4. Henry James, Preface to *The Spoils of Poynton*, in *The Art of the Novel*, ed. R. P. Blackmur (New York: Charles Scribner's Sons, 1937), p. 120.
5. James focuses here on the difficulty of establishing an acceptable relation to his reader, but that relationship is complicated by his kinship with his precursors. The necessity for organizing an "ado" is partially the result of the influence of Shakespeare, Eliot, and Turgenieff who have faced similar problems.
6. Georg Simmel, *The Philosophy of Money*, trans. Tom Bottomore and David Frisby (London, Henley and Boston: Routledge & Kegan Paul, 1978), pp. 212–17.
7. Henry James, "Honoré De Balzac," in *Notes on Novelists* (New York: Charles Scribner's Sons, 1914), p. 118.
8. "The Future of the Novel," pp. 182, 183.
9. Simmel, pp. 237–38.
10. Simmel, pp. 212–16.
11. I am indebted here to Marc Shell's useful discussion of Plato and money in *The Economy of Literature* (Baltimore: The Johns Hopkins University Press, 1978), pp. 36–62.
12. Tony Tanner, "The Fearful Self: Henry James's *The Portrait of a Lady*," in *Henry James: Modern Judgements*, ed. Tony Tanner (London: Macmillan, 1969), p. 143.
13. Henry James, "The Lesson of Balzac," in *The Question of Our Speech* (Boston: The Riverside Press, 1905), p. 93.
14. Henry James, "The Art of Fiction," in *Selected Literary Criticism*, p. 150.
15. Henry James, "Alphonse Daudet," in *Partial Portraits* (Ann Arbor: The University of Michigan Press, 1970), pp. 227–28.
16. "The Art of Fiction," pp. 50–51.
17. "The Art of Fiction," p. 54.
18. Preface to *The Princess Casamassima*, p. 65.
19. "The Art of Fiction," p. 54.
20. "The Lesson of Balzac," p. 71.
21. "The Lesson of Balzac," p. 92.
22. "Emile Zola," in *Notes on Novelists*, p. 60.
23. "The Future of the Novel," p. 188.
24. "The Art of Fiction," p. 57.
25. Preface to *The Princess Casamassima*, pp. 64–65.
26. For a different but suggestive reading of James's view of representation see Laurence B. Holland, *The Expense of Vision* (Princeton: Princeton University Press, 1964), pp. 120–38. Holland's reading of the *Portrait* emphasizes the analogy between writing and representational painting.
27. I am indebted here to Geoffrey H. Hartman's discussion of this problem in "Christopher Smart's 'Magnificat': Toward a Theory of Representation," in *The Fate of Reading* (Chicago: University of Chicago Press, 1975), pp. 74–75.
28. *The Expense of Vision*, pp. 121–22.
29. Henry James, *Hawthorne* (New York: Doubleday & Company, n.d.), p. 57.

30. Preface to *The Princess Casamassima*, p. 64.
31. Percy Lubbock, ed. *The Letters of Henry James* (New York: Charles Scribner's Sons, 1920), Vol. I, 142.
32. Preface to *The Spoils of Poynton*, p. 120.
33. "The Future of the Novel," p. 181.
34. "The Art of Fiction," p. 53.
35. Preface to *The Awkward Age*, p. 106.
36. *Letters*, I, 325.
37. "London Notes," in *Notes on Novelists*, p. 436.
38. "The Future of the Novel," p. 182.
39. "Alphonse Daudet," pp. 227–28.
40. Preface to *The Princess Casamassima*, p. 65.
41. Preface to *The Ambassadors*, p. 317.
42. "The Lesson of Balzac," p. 102.
43. "Alphonse Daudet," p. 227.
44. "The Future of the Novel," p. 188.

The Bought Generation: Another Look at Money in *The Sun Also Rises*
Patrick D. Morrow
Auburn University

> "Last week he tried to commit suicide," one waiter said.
> "Why?"
> "He was in despair."
> "About what?"
> "Nothing."
> "How do you know it was nothing?"
> "He has plenty of money."
>
> Ernest Hemingway, " A Clean, Well-Lighted Place"

For almost a generation now, critics have noted the importance of money in *The Sun Also Rises*.[1] In his 1963 Twayne United States Authors Series book on Hemingway, Earl Rovit proposed that the hierarchy of the characters' financial values correlated exactly with the hierarchy of their moral values.[2] This idea has been widely accepted. Claire Sprague in a 1969 article supports this argument, noting that in *The Sun Also Rises* "how one gets and spends money becomes a subject index to character. . . ."[3] Sprague also asserts that Jake "chooses to believe in value, chooses to erect a rigorous personal code which his literal account-keeping parallels."[4] Richard Sugg's 1972 article, "Hemingway, Money, and *The Sun Also Rises*," agrees with and amplifies the above, then moves on to explain how Hemingway uses financial transactions to reveal Jake as the novel's uncontested moral hero.[5] Finally, in a 1979 article, Nancy Comley proffers a diagrammed schemata "to show how this concern with money manifests itself in an economic structure of exchange values which the Hemingway hero learns to apply to his life, most especially to his emotional relationships."[6] This linear critical development has certainly provided worthwhile insights into the role of money in *The Sun Also Rises*, but the topic is hardly a closed account.

Money is not merely an issue or a revealing metaphorical and moral pattern in *The Sun Also Rises*; money is an obsession in this novel. By my count, *The Sun Also Rises* contains 142 direct references to money, including such varied forms of monetary transactions as paying bills, tipping, betting, bribery, and borrowing and lending, in addition to several metaphorical uses and philosophical discussions of money (see Appendix). That is a rate of almost one direct monetary reference for every other page in the Scribner paperback edition of the novel.[7] By my count there are an additional 71 indirect references, such as characters ordering drinks without direct mention of paying for them. In *The Sun Also Rises*, then, there is some kind of monetary reference for every 1.2 pages.[8] Two questions arise at once from this data: what would account for Hemingway's intense concern with money in *The Sun Also Rises*, and what is the meaning of money in this novel?

As Carlos Baker's biography, *Ernest Hemingway: A Life Story*, clearly reveals, Hemingway's mind was much on money during the composition period of *The Sun Also Rises* (1925–26).[9] For years he had been under parental scrutiny and fire for not settling down to a reliable job that would provide a good, decent living.[10] Ernest, however, was much more his parents' child than they realized. Young Hemingway was very concerned with receiving monetary validation for his short fiction as well as gaining favorable contractual arrangements for future novel-length works. On the two trips to Pamplona that Hemingway made during these years, he became very intrigued with the "fiesta" mentality of deferred financial and moral maintenance. His new friends, Harold Loeb, Lady Duff Twysden, Don Stewart, Pat Guthrie, and Kitty Cannell, indulged in a constant round of party now, pay later. This all must have been both very attractive and very shocking to Ernest Hemingway, middle class midwestern young man. The dissipates he had seen earlier in Paris and Germany were faceless fools; these people were his friends and confidantes. The esoteric Duff Twysden not only shadowed Hemingway during this period, but twice in secret messages requested large sums of money from him. Whether or not he gave her any francs is unknown, but she was paid off by being the unmistakable main model for Lady Brett.[11] Hemingway's attitude toward these people was, as Malcolm Cowley said of the expatriates' attitude toward their war experiences, "spectatorial."[12]

Hemingway's other financial dealings through these years indicate his resistance to *carpe diem*, to speculative or spendthrift behavior. He damn well intended to work hard making a good living writing—not what people wanted to read, but what he knew to be truth. During this period Hemingway also first developed his natural talent for driving a hard bargain coupled with an unerring eye for the good deal. Without an agent, and with only *In Our Time* for collateral, he shrewdly played Knopf, Harcourt, and Boni and Liveright against each other to secure a fine financial arrangement for *The Sun Also Rises* from yet another publisher, Charles Scribner.[13]

Hemingway's guilty break-up with wife Hadley began during the writing of *The Sun Also Rises*, and there may have been a financial dimension to their split. The direct cause of the Ernest-Hadley break-up was Hemingway's second wife, Pauline Pfeiffer, whom Baker describes as a *Vogue* fashion editor searching Paris for a husband, the eldest daughter of "a landowning squire in Piggott, Arkansas."[14] In addition, Pauline's multi-millionaire and childless Uncle Gus took a strong liking to Ernest even before meeting him.[15] Was it from sympathy, guilt, or both that Hemingway assigned all immediate and future royalties from *The Sun Also Rises* to Hadley and their son? As we read through Baker's biography, Hemingway's attraction to what Auden called "the parish of rich women"[16] becomes all too evident. Nasty, satirical, and complex, *The Sun Also Rises* has a definite autobiographical dimension, and money loomed as a large and disturbing issue for Hemingway in 1925–26. Thus the beginning of Hemingway's life-long monetary conflict, pointedly summarized by Scott Donaldson: "On the one hand, [Hemingway] learned from his environment that it was right and manly to make money. . . . On the other hand, Hemingway had also been indoctrinated to think that easy money could ruin a man."[17]

Perceived as recurring metaphorical pattern, the monetary references in *The Sun Also Rises* reveal not only a vertical, hierarchical objective correlative to character morality, but also a constant circular, senseless, and frustrating motion by the characters. As such, money is a major component of the novel's circular formal and thematic essence. Its story is about a circle of people who journey in a circle within a circle (Paris, San Sebastain, Bayonne, Pamplona, Burguete, Pamplona, Burguete, Pamplona, San Sebastian, Madrid, Paris). Circular objects, from lights and tables to coins to the bull ring, form much of the setting. Hemingway even puns on this metaphor with his constant references to rounds of drinks. Money establishes the moral dimension of *The Sun Also Rises* as circular.

A whirl of speculation is the order of the day in *The Sun Also Rises*. Despite all the buying and selling of goods, the money spent buys few articles of substance. Expensive and frequent purchases of alcohol lubricate this *La Dolce Vita* world where everybody parties, but no one has any fun. Like alcohol, transportation is purchased for diversion, and throughout the novel there are several aimless taxi cab and automobile rides. At least transportation does provide movement to a new hotel room or café for the old diversions. There are no investments in the novel, and the monetary waste is continual, increasingly appalling as the novel progresses. While the concept of making money is mentioned several times in *The Sun Also Rises*, there is *no* mention of money in terms of future security. Rather, more money ensures that the "entertaining" circular movement of life without purpose can continue.

Several ideas about money recur during the course of *The Sun Also Rises*. One is the idea that money is the way to buy and control friendship. For example, Robert Cohn offers to pay Jake's way to South America (p. 10). The rich Cohn defines himself largely by using money as magnanimous gesture, a way to obligate, to control. Similarly, Count (another Hemingway pun?) Mippipopolous offers Brett ten thousand dollars if she will accompany him to Biarritz (p. 33). "The high priest of materialism," as Delbert E. Wylder calls the Count,[18] wishes to join and encumber the younger generation by financial obligation. With more success, Brett buys the friendship of Jake's concierge for two hundred francs (p. 55). A desperate Pedro Romero presses money on Brett in the hope of establishing physical control and obligation over her (p. 242). In addition to subsidizing Brett, Jake overtips at a hotel in order to buy the help's friendship in case he should happen to stay there again (p. 233). Money is the key link among the novel's characters, their primary foundation for establishing relationships.

Even art and religion are measured in terms of money in *The Sun Also Rises*. Robert Cohn writes, according to Jake, a very bad novel, but ironically Jake is impressed that the book made so much money (p. 8). Jake also admires Bill Gorton because of all the money he has made on his books (p. 70). No mention is made about the quality of Gorton's writing. Journalist Jake writes for money to buy time for indulging in seemingly masochistic diversions. Jake, who professes to be Catholic, goes to a church where he quite sincerely prays to make a lot of money (p. 97). When he mentions money in the prayer, though, he loses track of his prayer (as he has lost track of his faith), and becomes ashamed of himself. The bullfighters Belmonte and Mercial have corrupted their art for money (pp. 214–15); Romero is the true artist, not connected at all with money—until his encounter with Brett. Most of the characters at one time or another believe in and act on the notion that money purchases exemption from personal and moral responsibilities.

The only chapter in which money is not a factor is Chapter Twelve, where Jake and Bill go on a fishing trip to Burguete. Money does get mentioned early in the chapter when Bill inquires after he has seen Jake digging for worms, " 'What were you doing? Burying your money?' " (p. 113). This is exactly what Jake has done; he buries all mention of money during their trip to the Irati River. Hemingway chooses to show nature as incorrupted in this section, a healing wilderness for troubled men. The stream, as a non-circular encounter between man and nature, is one place where money has no use or value.

This pastoral interlude or counter-action in *The Sun Also Rises* supposedly features the novel's one truly admirable character, Wilson-Harris.[19] He actually functions, however, not as a minor code hero, but as an echo of Jake's worst characteristics. Duplicitous as his name reveals, Wilson-Harris insists on buying friendship with alcohol (p. 128) and gifts (p. 130). He makes what should be at least for Jake a brutally ironic statement: " 'I say. You don't know what it's meant to me to have you chaps up here . . . . I've not had much fun since the war' " (p. 129). Ever the affected Englishman, fawning continual compliments, Wilson-Harris is defined by his sentimental loneliness. His congeniality masks the magnanimous gestures of a man who pays to keep Jake and Bill for himself. Not surprisingly, Wilson-Harris declines an invitation to return to "civilization" and join the circle for the festival.

Money serves as a continual means for Hemingway to define and develop his characters within their circles of frustration. Narrator Jake Barnes, mutilated by a grotesque war accident, feels sexual desire, but is physically incapable of having sex.[20] Money appears to be Jake's only means for overcoming his impotence and achieving some measure of power. He pays the majority of the expenses in the book and is also the prime lender; rarely is he repaid in cash. To Lady Brett Ashley, his primary client, he gives all that he possibly can, and is compensated by her off-hand requests for more and more financial support. As the various café scenes indicate, money is typically the medium for their emotional exchanges. Jake even grants money sacred sanction and authority by substituting money for grace in the first church scene (p. 97). Jake may be so obsessed with money partially because he sees its function in an honest perspective. Without money, he and the other "cult" members would have absolute *nada*; with it, there are at least amusing diversions and some measure of feeling.

Jake's sidekick, Bill Gorton, is more bemused visitor than loyal group member. Only loosely an expatriate, he is also the only member of the party not emotionally involved with Brett. Bill does express some interest in Edna, the tourist and "groupie" picked up in a Pamplona bar. She has known Bill before, and acts most impressed with his apparently independent ways and means. But Bill's real interests and values lie elsewhere. Gorton is a financially successful nature writer, and his behavior at the fiesta demonstrates his eager willingness to enjoy the corruption of civilization and success. Bill's monetary philosophy can best be established by his own words: " 'Simple exchange of values. You give them money. They give you a stuffed dog' " (p. 72). Money equals value; money *is* value.

In Pamplona, Jake continues to buy and Lady Brett enjoys being purchased. Not valuing loyalty very highly, throughout the novel Brett entertains herself by the way a variety of men speculate over her. She uses Robert Cohn and Pedro Romero, and then sells them out by repossessing herself. She uses Mike Campbell as something of a sympatico sponge and reliable sexual toy while maintaining Jake as a crying towel and source of instant income. She could be considered parasitic, living off three men's money in the same careless manner in which she employs their bodies and attentions. Brett is the group's prostitute in that most all her relationships sooner or later become based on money. Her "intended," Mike Campbell, is both a financial and moral bankrupt. He too lives on credit, continually depending on his friends to bail him out of embarrassing situations. A practiced free-loader, Campbell even manages to have Brett pay most of his Pamplona hotel bill (p. 230). Mike hints that he was cheated monetarily by his former partner, just as in Pamplona he is cheated emotionally by Brett (p. 79). Mike whines and whines, the complete, even willing professional victim. As deadbeat, Brett takes the opposite tack, protesting loudly against her most insistent emotional and financial creditor, Robert Cohn.

The other two men in Brett's life besides Jake and Mike, Robert Cohn and Pedro Romero, fancy themselves idealists, but actually find their fulfillment as well in being victims. Cohn is a corrupted idealist, smugly believing that no one appreciates his true worth. He plays a system of romantic chivalry with the group, expecting and receiving ridicule and rejection. At the same time, Cohn attempts to proffer money as a way to obligate other characters, and as a way to rid himself of problems, such as how to placate his enraged fiancée in order to have a seacoast fling with Brett. Once again, money resolves a difficult personal and moral situation in *The Sun Also Rises* (p. 49). The immature Cohn is concerned with appearances and "getting away with it," shunning substantial values at all cost. Of course Cohn, the sad, ineffectual woman-haunted Princetonian, is most debilitated by being a Scott Fitzgerald hero in an Ernest Hemingway novel. As the logical polar opposite to Cohn, Pedro Romero appears at first to be incorrupt and incorruptible. However, he picks up enough of Lost Generation life to realize the potential in Brett's passion for him. When Romero finds that he cannot possess Brett, he finds a mutually agreeable indirect means of payment for services rendered. He, too, comes to know how these expatriates value money.

The circular movement of money and characters in *The Sun Also Rises* positions Jake and Brett as antagonists at the center in the novel's ring of action. An initiation novel *The Sun Also Rises* is not. Both these antagonists have been wounded, and out of their experiences have developed clearly defined moral codes. Brett believes in and acts on extrinsic values, a code of survival through sensation and appetite. As Brett puts it, "I've always done just what I wanted" (p. 184). Brett values not abstract concepts but what she wants to have. She accepts the depravity of man, exists only in the present tense, lives for disorder and uproar, and, as a creature of process, values most what she cannot have. But Brett also possesses a compelling contrary dimension, a great capacity for nurturing and love, and she is never more human and appealing than when she exhibits this vulnerability.

In terms of character development and values, the issue of money reveals much about Brett Ashley, Jake's formidable love and opponent. Robert Cohn first sees her as a lovely creature resembling Snow White (p. 39), then views her, with Mike's drunken approval, as Circe (p. 144). Jake typically sees her as the irresistible tormentor, fate, the bitch goddess. Critics frequently lose objectivity with Brett and empathize with these male characters' feelings about her. For example, Sheridan Baker states that "Brett must have an ever new man [sic] to replace the one she drains,"[21] and Robert W. Lewis portrays Brett as the woman in Ecclesiastes whose "heart is snares and nets."[22] Brett, however, has her own values, and it is the males' continual egocentric mistake of substituting their own projections of Brett's identity for her actual identity that causes so much masculine misery in the novel. Highlighted by contrast to Edna and Frances, Lady Brett is defined not by men, but by her own self-validated morality of appetite and survival. Brett is the best and most powerful practitioner of traditional male values, and this strength is nowhere more in evidence than when the males insist on celebrating her as their female goddess (p. 155). The *riau-riau* establishes Brett's complete control of the situation. Hardly a passive female, alternating between feeling states of male adoration and self-martyrdom, Brett surrounds herself with male strays who define themselves by being dominated victims.

Hemingway is aware of the humor this role-reversal situation can provide. We note the following exchange between Brett and Jake in the Café Select.

> I [Jake] said good night to Brett at the bar. The count [Mippipopolous] was buying champagne. "Will you take a glass with us, sir?" he asked.
> "No. Thanks awfully. I have to go."
> "Really going?" Brett asked.
> "Yes," I said. "I've got a rotten headache." (p. 29)

Jake will come to imitate more than Brett's British speech mannerisms. Established early in *The Sun Also Rises*, Brett's ability to generate, sustain, and be the center of situation after situation borders on the charismatic. Brett's outrageous behavior, her wardrobe and hair style, her calling herself a "chap," her skill and pride in being a "good drunk," her cavalier assumption that she can always get money—all demonstrate the validity of her strategy that to be a successful female, one must compete to be the most successful male.

Brett seeks not happiness but freedom. To this end she willingly rents herself out to attractive and useful landlords, but she is dominated and bought by no man. True to her values, she never once accepts money as payment for sex. Brett views the prostitute Georgette with scorn, nastily calling Jake's evening with her "restraint of trade" (p. 22). The novel's absorbing and futile quest by the leading male characters to become sole owner of Lady Ashley climaxes with her rejection of Pedro Romero. Like the other males, Romero is capable of seeing only his personal projection of Brett, but not Brett. He wishes to make an honest woman of her, reforming her by means of marriage, motherhood, and long hair. As Brett tells Jake near the end of *The Sun Also Rises*:

"I didn't know whether I could make him go, and I didn't have a sou to go away and leave him. He tried to give me a lot of money, you know. I told him I had scads of it. He knew that was a lie. I couldn't take his money, you know. . . . He really wanted to marry me. So I couldn't go away from him, he said. He wanted to make it sure I could never go away from him. After I'd gotten more womanly, of course." (p. 242)

Brett typically acts in the plural; she sends for Jake, but plans a return to Mike Campbell. Brett tells Jake she is not a bitch and " 'It's sort of what we have instead of God' " (p. 245) partially because she would like to believe these words, but especially because she likes Jake, is sensitive to his problems, and knows he needs to hear this. More than any character in the novel, Brett has the capability to balance a show of pity and irony. Jake celebrates his quasi-repossession by indulging his appetite and by buying Brett all the booze she can drink and food she can eat. Brett intimidates and disorients the male characters in *The Sun Also Rises* to such an extent that none of them thinks to analyze her motives and behavior with the intention of developing effective strategies for either friendship or revenge.

As Brett's antagonist, Jake, with his capacity for being nurtured, believes in the intrinsic values of the *aficion*: purity and skill are inherently beautiful and good. With a shaky faith, he wants and needs to believe in loyalty, justice, love, and the fundamental good will of mankind. We note the careful accounting of his bank balance (p. 30), his notion of fair payment (p. 148), and realize that he is the party of order. But Jake's vulnerability is his contradictory attraction to and need for the dominating Brett Ashley and her values. This vulnerability exists because Jake has been so terribly wounded. A Catholic, however fallen-away, he knows that he must have done something terribly wrong to have received such a punishment. Having no idea what he did to deserve this *corida*, Jake sometimes manufactures evil—betraying Montoya, pimping, getting drunk, acceding to Brett—in an attempt to believe that behind his being wounded, cause and effect firmly stand. Thus, Jake can perceive himself as an evil hero. However sympathetic or admirable, Jake is badly debilitated. This is a Fisher King, not an heroic young knight, that Hemingway sends into the arena to do battle against Duessa.

It *is* rather pleasant to think that after the fiesta, Jake recovers his lost values while vacationing in San Sebastian, so that when he encounters Brett in Madrid, he has come to his senses with a self-awareness born out of tragic recognition, and can rise above further involvement in her romantic conspiracies. As we have seen, such forms the prevailing critical view. Hemingway himself insisted that *The Sun Also Rises* was not a satire but a tragedy.[23] If Hemingway's book follows the tragic novel convention of a fallen, wounded hero rising to self-knowledge, a morally admirable perspective, and a consequent series of actions, then Jake must be congratulated for achieving an heroic stature in the *dénouement*. However, partially through the money metaphor, Hemingway undercuts this uplifting pattern to reveal not an emerging hero, but a continuation of frustration in this world where extrinsic values dominate. Drunk in Pamplona, Jake muses about money and life, ending his reverie by stating: "Maybe if you found out how to live in it you learned from that what it was all about" (p. 148). Jake comes to realize that "how to live in it" (extrinsic values, i.e., money) and "what it was all about" (intrinsic values, i.e., honor) are at irreconcilable odds. Like Krebs of "Soldier's Home," Jake resigns himself to being overwhelmed by a stronger force (Brett). Hemingway's pronouncement on *The Sun Also Rises* as a tragedy rings true when we realize the tragedy of the novel is that Jake cannot act on his beliefs. Typical of the twentieth-century American novelist, Hemingway saves most of the blow from this realization not for his protagonist, but for his audience.

In the opening of Part III, the scene immediately following the Pamplona festival's ending, Jake makes a number of decisions that indicate not resolve or enlightenment, but a serious depression. First of all, he determinedly insists on staying alone in San Sebastian, the scene of the earlier Cohn-Ashley "crime." Interestingly, although Jake notes that he has been to this hotel before (p. 234), he never names the hotel, possibly because while there, Jake acts like a sanitarium patient rather than a spa vacationer. Jake is comforted by watching the visiting nurses, immediately imposes a daily routine of therapeutic swimming and sitting, and refuses to join the community of bicycle racers. Jake's self-absorption is overwhelming. Typical of institutional life, meals constitute the high points of his days. He acts drugged and tense, at the edge of breakdown, not unlike Nick in "Big Two-Hearted River." Jake's languid days of isolated insulation do afford protection against the outside world of Spain, where "you could not tell about anything" (pp. 233–34). His regrets about returning to Spain concern consequences, phrased in a nostalgic financial metaphor about France.

> Everything is on such a clear financial basis in France. It is the simplest country to live in. No one makes things complicated by becoming your friend

for any obscure reason. If you want people to like you you have only to spend a little money. (p. 233)

When Brett's telegrams arrive, Jake laments "that meant San Sebastian all shot to hell" (p. 239). This expression of surprise is an act. Having learned from Mike Campbell that Brett is broke (p. 230), Jake knows that she will be in touch with him shortly. Certainly Jake could wire Brett to go to hell and continue his quasi-hospitalization, but like an heroic rescue agent, he rushes to her aid at once. Again, action is " 'put on the bill' " (p. 239). What Brett does need is a paying audience. Page after page she has demonstrated her ability to rescue herself.

Far from establishing a clean, well-lighted place of heroic action for Jake, the final scene ironically demonstrates the novel's enduring French values: *plus ça change, plus c'est la même chose.* What does the last scene change except location? In Madrid, Jake still pays and Brett still buys. When Jake first meets Brett in the sleazy Hotel Montana, he notes that her "room was in that disorder produced only by those who have always had servants" (p. 241). Jake continues his role of servant par excellence by patiently listening to Brett's sad tale of her latest affair; by paying for drinks and meals; and by booking them on the Sud Express for a night trip back to Paris. Jake would have paid for Brett's room, but Romero has already made this contribution as Brett's severance payment.[24] At Botin's, "one of the best restaurants in the world" (p. 245), Brett becomes concerned with Jake's sudden conspicuous consumption (including five bottles of *rioja alta*), fearing another unpleasant scene of drunken, weepy pouting (cf. pp. 54–56). Brett soothes by words but abuses by actions, a much more effective strategy for achieving her goals than the explosion of verbal indictment that Frances practices. In the end, both Jake and Robert Cohn "take it." The final tipping, the furtive taxi ride, and that hideously ironic upraised baton of the mounted policeman establish at the novel's finalé not a sense of recognition or resolution, but a continuing wandering. Like Francesca and Paolo, swept on hot winds without touching through their circle of Dante's Hell, Jake and Brett are driven through summertime Madrid on the winds of money. Instead of establishing security in space, money in *The Sun Also Rises* is most useful for killing time. Rather than establishing superiority or even disengagement, Jake capitulates by joining Brett and her extrinsic values of meaningless motion and immediate gratification.

The use of money, then, is a major means for Hemingway to show the corruption of this modern world where values are relative, transitory, and for sale. Far from praising this lost generation, Hemingway damns their meaningless exchanges and lack of purpose, the absence of a moral center in their world. He attacks their irresponsibility by dramatizing their fruitless, circular quests for happy diversions. Jake requires diversion to forget his faded Catholicism and his painfully impotent love for Brett. Brett requires diversion to cover up her exploitations and encroaching middle age. Mike needs diversion because he is both a moral and financial bankrupt; diversions occupy his time and give some vague sense of direction to his life, namely a moving on to wherever he can still obtain credit. While a means, money is not—as Bill Gorton claims—an end in *The Sun Also Rises*. Despite the many equations of money to value in the book, money is not in itself valuable to the characters, but only the means for continuing their dissipation. If money is not a value in itself, if it is not a center for *this* group, then Hemingway's characters literally have lost all values. Far from being hostages to fortune, these characters, however wounded, create their own tragedy and hell.

The Sun Also Rises is a cyclical, cynical young man's book. Jake, Brett, and, by insinuation, Mike are the only characters left at the end of the novel because, in spite of their singular and collective guilt, they all accept and function well in the never-ending cycle of borrowing on time. Neither of the romantics, Robert Cohn and Pedro Romero, ever comprehends this cycle: they are both idealists, albeit corrupt ones. Bill Gorton is eliminated from the cycle because he is only a visiting expatriate, soon off to America. The concept of "paying the bill" works in tandem with the novel's cyclical process. Jake pays for his impotence and loss of religion; Brett pays for her manipulative behavior; Mike, Cohn and Romero pay for thinking they can possess Brett; Mike pays for his insolvent status; Cohn pays for behaving badly; Bill Gorton pays for his stagnancy. All the characters pay for their lack of purpose, their lack of definite goals, and their values which center around vanities.

Payment in *The Sun Also Rises* is not rendered in such concrete terms as cold cash; rather, the characters are mortgaged to frustration. As this cyclical pattern indicates, appropriately consummated by Jake's tipping a waiter and ordering a taxi as the novel closes, these characters can never gain on their moral deficit, but shall continue, gradually and voluntarily, to slide into the self-destruction of a material and moral receivership.

NOTES

1. In addition to the critics noted, Scott Donaldson has an extensive analysis of Hemingway and money in *By Force of Will: The Life and Art of Ernest Hemingway* (New York: Viking, 1977), pp. 10–59.
2. Earl Rovit, *Ernest Hemingway* (New York: Twayne, 1963), pp. 151–52.
3. Claire Sprague, "*The Sun Also Rises*: Hemingway's 'Clear Financial Basis,'" *American Quarterly*, 21 (Summer 1969), 259.
4. Sprague, 265.
5. Richard P. Sugg, "Hemingway, Money, and *The Sun Also Rises*," *Fitzgerald-Hemingway Annual*, (1972) (Washington, D.C.: NCR/Microcard Editions), pp. 257–67.
6. Nancy Comley, "Hemingway: The Economics of Survival," *Novel*, 12 (Spring 1979), 244.
7. Ernest Hemingway, *The Sun Also Rises* (New York: Charles Scribner's Sons, 1954). All further references to *The Sun Also Rises* are from this edition; pages cited are included in the text. I am indebted to my English 352 class (Fall, 1977) for first showing me the extent to which monetary references appear in *The Sun Also Rises*.
8. *The Sun Also Rises*, of course, was written under the shadow of *The Great Gatsby*, the most famous modern novel about the American obsession with money. Hemingway's next novel, *A Farewell to Arms*, rarely has any mention of money.
9. Carlos Baker, *Hemingway: A Life Story* (New York: Bantam, 1970), pp. 197–229.
10. Donaldson, p. 15.
11. Baker, p. 202.
12. Malcolm Cowley, *Exiles' Return* (New York: Viking, 1951), p. 38.
13. Baker, pp. 210–11.
14. Baker, p. 184.
15. Baker, pp. 246, 260.
16. W. H. Auden, "In Memory of W. B. Yeats," *The Collected Poems of W. H. Auden* (New York: Random House, 1945), p. 50.
17. Donaldson, pp. 58–59.
18. Delbert E. Wylder, *Hemingway's Heroes* (Albuquerque: The University of New Mexico Press, 1969), p. 61.
19. Gerald T. Gordon, "Hemingway's Wilson-Harris: The Search for Value in *The Sun Also Rises*," *Fitzgerald-Hemingway Annual* (1972) (Washington D.C.: NCR/Microcard Editions), pp. 237–44.
20. See George Plimpton, "An Interview with Ernest Hemingway," *The Paris Review*, 18 (Spring 1958), 76–77.
21. Sheridan Baker, *Ernest Hemingway: An Introduction and Interpretation* (New York: Barnes and Noble, 1967), p. 50.
22. Robert W. Lewis, *Hemingway: The Art of Love* (Austin: University of Texas Press, 1965), p. 34.
23. In a letter to Maxwell Perkins, dated November 19, 1926, Hemingway stated that *The Sun Also Rises* was not "a hollow or bitter satire, but a damn tragedy. . . ." Quoted in Carlos Baker, *Hemingway: The Writer as Artist* (Princeton, N.J.: Princeton University Press, 1956), p. 81.
24. Hemingway may have used the name "Pedro Romero" not only in honor of the first great Spanish bullfighter, but because Romero is a common Sephardic name. The subtle irony of casting *both* Cohn and Romero as Jews would likely have appealed to young Hemingway's sense of humor.

APPENDIX

Direct References to Money in *The Sun Also Rises*

Ref. No.	Page No.	
		Book I
1	4	Jake tells of Cohn losing most of his first fortune.
2	5	Cohn establishes small "review of the Arts" with remnants of his fortune; the magazine becomes too expensive.
3	5	Cohn's mother has given him a $300 per month allowance.
4	6	Cohn buys a newspaper.
5	9	Cohn gambles and wins big at bridge.
6	9	Cohn reads *The Purple Land* "as though it had been an R. G. Dun report."
7	9	Jake turns down Cohn's proposed trip to South America: "Too expensive."
8	10	Cohn offers to pay Jake's way to South America.
9	10	Jake notes that Cohn has "plenty of money."
10	15	With Georgette, Jake pays for several "saucers."
11	17	Georgette notes about artists: "Still, some of them make money."
12	22	Brett arrives: "I say, give a chap a brandy and soda."
13	22	Jake refers to his evening as "priceless."
14	22	Referring to Jake spending the evening with Georgette, Brett says: "It's in restraint of trade."
15	23	Jake leaves a 55 franc note in an envelope for Georgette.
16	24	Jake tips a waiter.
17	26	Brett: "Don't we pay for the things we do, though? . . . I'm paying for it all now."
18	28	Jake pays for a taxi ride with Brett.
19	29	Count Mippipopolous buys champagne.
20	30	Jake works on his bank statement.
21	32	Brett discusses where the Count got his money.
22	32	Brett states that the Count is "putting up" (i.e., supporting) the artist, Zizi.
23	33	Brett reports that the Count offered her $10,000 to go with him to Biarritz or another spa.
24	35	A street vendor urges tourists to buy his wares.

25	37	Jake offers Krum two francs for a taxi ride.
26	38	Jake notes that Mike Campbell will "be rich as hell some day."
27	42	Jake notes that Harvey Stone won 200 francs from him when they gambled.
28	42	Harvey laments that his money hasn't come.
29	42	Jake gives Harvey 100 francs.
30	46	Frances notes that she does not "have enough money to lunch at the Ritz."
31	46	Jake buys the latest *Paris Times*.
32	47	Frances notes that, in giving up alimony to obtain a speedy divorce, she has no money. Cohn, she notes, does have money.
33	48	Cohn will give Frances 200 pounds.
34	49	Frances reacts to this severance payment.
35	49	Frances states that her mother put all her money into French war bonds.
36	53	Mme. Duzinell had once "owned a drink-selling concession."
37	54	Brett reports giving Jake's concierge 200 francs.
38	56	Brett praises the Count's willingness to buy champagne.
39	57	The Count notes that having a title "costs you money."
40	57	Brett explains about her title: "I've had hell's own amount of credit on mine."
41	60	The Count notes that he received two arrow wounds while on a business trip to Abyssinia.
42	60	The Count advises: "You must get to know the values."
43	62	The Count muses: "I get more value for my money in old brandy than in any other antiquities."
44	62	Dinner and drinks on the Count.
45	63	Brett notes that Mike Campbell's mother is going to "put up" (i.e., finance) his divorce.
46	63	Brett: "Michael's people have loads of money."
47	63	The Count admits to supporting Zizi, "but I don't want to have him around."
48	64	Jake offers to pay for their drinks, but the Count insists on paying.
49	65	Jake tips the chauffeur twenty francs.

Book II

50	69	Cohn notes that he can always be reached through his bankers.
51	70	Bill "had made a lot of money on his last book, and he was going to make a lot more."
52	71	Bill tells of trying to secure a black fighter's money in Vienna.
53	71	The fighter refused to be bribed.
54	72	The fighter promised to return the money Bill loaned him.
55	73	"Simple exchange of values," a pie-eyed Bill notes.
56	74	Mme. Lecomte hopes she will be rich.
57	77	Dinner.
58	79	Brett notes that a "chap" bought her the celebrated slouch hat.
59	79	Brett says that she and Mike have money (ironic), followed by her wry comment: "Mr. Campbell is an undischarged bankrupt."
60	79	Mike notes that his ex-partner bought him a farewell drink.
61	82	Brett and Mike will go to Pamplona if their money comes.
62	82	Jake notes that Bill will not need to buy a fishing rod.
63	84	Mike and Brett expect their money the next day.
64	85	Bill and Jake bribe porter (unsuccessfully) on the train.
65	87	Bill and Jake pay for wine and sandwiches plus tip.
66	87	Bill and Jake buy a bottle of wine.
67	90	Bill does need a fishing rod, so one is purchased, plus two landing-nets.
68	91	Car is hired.
69	91	Gambling for beers (probably paid for by Cohn).
70	91	Hotel payment is rendered.
71	94	Driver is paid.
72	95	Bill bets Cohn on Brett's arrival; discussion of the bet.
73	96	Jake checks on his bull-fight subscription and finds it paid up.
74	96	Jake tips a porter.
75	97	Jake prays for money in a church.

MONEY IN *THE SUN ALSO RISES*

76	98	Cohn says the bet on Brett's arrival is off. Cohn would like to bet on the outcome of a bull-fight.
77	99	Of bull-fights, Jake notes: "You don't need any economic interest."
78	99	Jake buys three bus tickets to Burguete.
79	100	Cohn reimburses Jake for bus ticket.
80	106	Drinks, and a misunderstanding with the tip (Bill and Jake).
81	106	Drinks (with the Basques).
82	107	In America, Jake says, good wine is available if you pay for it.
83	109	Jake and the inn manager discuss Burguete hotel rates; they agree on a price.
84	113	Bill inquires if Jake is burying his money.
85	115	Bill says: "One group claims women support you."
86	123	"You're in the pay of the Anti-Saloon League."
87	124	Bill: "All our biggest business men have been dreamers."
88	127	Jake tips young lady who delivers a telegram.
89	128	Cohn's cheapness with the telegram is noted.
90	128	Jake and Bill pay for a telegram to Cohn.
91	129	Wilson-Harris, Jake, and Bill purchase wine in a pub.
92	136	Mike discusses payment of his tailor.
93	136	Mike discusses his bankruptcy.
94	137	Drinks.
95	138	Price of wine advertised in a shop is discussed.
96	142	Mike says Cohn will buy a drink.
97	144	Brett wonders if drinks have been paid for.
98	148–49	Jake's "getting your money's worth" speech.
99	151	Café prices, before and during the festival.
100	156	Jake offers to pay for some wine, but is refused.
101	156–57	Jake buys two wine skins (botas).
102	157	Jake pays to fill the wine skins with wine.
103	157	A man buys Jake a drink.
104	159	Dinner (with prices doubled for the festival).
105	161	Jake gives "an extra ticket to a waiter to sell."
106	172	Montoya says some people "don't know what he's [Romero] worth."
107	172	Bill buys shoe-shines for Mike.

108	185	Romero wants Brett to tell him he'll be a millionaire.
109	185	Romero hopes that Brett's palm reading "sees" many bulls at a thousand duros apiece.
110	189	No one cares that Mike is a bankrupt.
111	189	Jake notes that people usually get bitter about money being owed them.
112	190	People wait in line to buy bull-fight tickets.
113	192	Edna and Mike discuss Mike's finances.
114	192	Mike announces that he borrowed 100 pesetas from Montoya.
115	195	People continue to wait for bull-fight tickets to go on sale.
116	200	Mike notes that his going into the bull-ring "wouldn't be fair to my creditors."
117	213	Belmonte gets 30,000 pesetas per bull-fight.
118	217	Crowd has paid for bull which turns out to be damaged, but they want to see it killed anyway.

Book III

119	228	Bill pays for lunch.
120	228	Hotel bill is paid.
121	229	Gambling for drinks in Biarritz.
122	229	Mike, without cash, discusses his financial situation.
123	230	Mike states that Brett paid most of his Pamplona hotel bill.
124	230	Bill loses the dice roll for drinks.
125	230	Mike thinks a drive will do his credit good.
126	231	Mike tells Jake to pay for the car, saying "I'll send you my share."
127	231–32	Jake and the chauffeur wrangle about the trip's cost.
128	232	Jake tips the chauffeur.
129	232	Jake buys a newspaper.
130	233	Jake overtips a waiter.
131	233	Jake says: "Everything is on such a clear financial basis in France."
132	234	Jake tips "everyone a little too much at the hotel to make more friends."
133	234	Train tickets for San Sebastian.

134	236	The bicycle racers find that: "The money could be arranged."
135	238	Jake pays for a bath cabin.
136	238	Jake tips the concierge for bringing a telegram.
137	239	The concierge waits for another tip.
138	239	Jake has his hotel stay and Sud Express trip "put on the bill."
139	242	Romero offers Brett money and she refuses it.
140	243	Brett and Jake discover that Romero has paid her hotel bill.
141	243	Jake "arranged for berths on the Sud Express for the night."
142	247	Jake tips the waiter for hailing a taxi.

Tales of Obscene Power: Money, Culture, and the Historical Fictions of E. L. Doctorow

David S. Gross
University of Oklahoma

As an interpretive code or theoretical orientation, the bundle of forces suggested by the subject of money and literature is frightening to me both in immensity and complexity. Especially to one who wishes to assert or defend the validity of a Marxist hermeneutic, the examination of literary production and signification from such a perspective seems to amount to an embarrassment of riches. Faced with that immensity, I choose to start with the embarrassment, following a hunch that I might find in a nervous reluctance to speak on this subject the most profitable way into it.

Fredric Jameson has described Marx's statement that "it is not the consciousness of men that determines their existence, but, on the contrary, their social being that determines their consciousness"[1] as an "ever-scandalous discovery."[2] What I want to propose is that the status of money in literature and in its interpretation, as in life, points us toward equally scandalous truths, truths which it has been the function of most modern approaches to literature to mystify or deny. Marx's discovery is offensive because it challenges some basic intellectual assumptions about the putative independence, integrity and lofty origins of consciousness and its productions of serious intent, from religion and philosophy to literature. It opens the forbidden area of materialist determination, threatening notions of consciousness and culture as a clean, privileged refuge from getting and spending, notions which seem to partake of the sacred for intellectuals in modern society. As Jameson goes on to say:

> This determination makes itself felt in the "deja-donné," which always transcends consciousness as given no matter how exhaustively it is assumed, just as it finds its visual representation in the geological deposits of language as script. Such a dimension might well be seen as the ultimate bedrock of the signified.[3]

I cannot go into the implications of this larger area here; there is not space in this discussion for either a defense or an explication of the thesis that "modes of production" and the social relations which are specific to them constitute crucially determining historical forces and that a recognition of that fact provides the most useful interpretive code for historical investigations.[4] Instead, I want to turn here to the related but narrower question of the power and significance of money, and of the complex repression of awareness of such meanings, the embarrassment I spoke of earlier. For while the importance of money in literature is obvious, to dwell on it seems somehow distasteful, and is likely to be denounced in the same terms in which Marx's scandalous discovery is so often dismissed: as stupid and/or inconsequential or as narrow, "vulgar" determinism.

It is a truism that money and sexual/romantic love constitute the central concerns of realist fiction. As Raymond Williams has pointed out in his discussion of British Restoration drama, the London marriage market for the scions of both old aristocratic and newly wealthy rural families points to a significant linking of the two themes which will persist both in drama and in fiction.[5] But Williams' most interesting observation in that regard comes in his discussion of ethical questions in Jane Austen's novels, where he sees a structure of feeling on this question which links her with George Eliot.

Implicitly in the earlier novelist and explicitly in Eliot, Williams sees as decisive an assertion that money and love are causally linked, with money the determining factor, and that this should not be so.[6] In that view, love and sexuality are seen as crucial aspects of human existence which should not be linked to money or used to manipulate people in aggressive, acquisitive desire. All matters of conduct and morality in such novels center around the question of whether principle (or authentic and generous desire) will prevail over money greed and its dominance in human relations. Austen and Eliot defend that classic humanist position that humans should be the measure of all things, and it is with real anguish that they come to the conclusion that gold, instead, provides that universal standard.

Thus of the two principal subjects of so much literature, it is much more respectable to assert the value and significance of love than money. Once beyond a certain idealist and archaic belles-lettrist prudishness, most critics do not want to deny the significance and suitability of the love-sex complex as both subject matter and central source for literature.

And if we assert that the prominence of such concerns in literature suggests or "reflects" its centrality in "real life," only the most purely formalist literary critics would be likely to object. The victory of depth psychology, especially in its discussion of dreams, desire and fantasy, is by now fairly clear in these areas. But, of course, not all reluctance or repugnance to speak of this area has vanished, and the traces that remain lead us to that more forbidden area, the enormous shaping power of money in our world and in its literature.

When money's power and significance are central subject matter in literature they are virtually always presented critically. The most cursory reading of the great nineteenth-century novels shows this to be true. And it is equally obvious that from Aristotle through Christ to twentieth-century social critics the power, prestige and privilege accorded to wealth in money has been consistently denounced. Now some small part of such criticism can be linked to the puritanical renunciations which underlie the pathological and compulsive enterprise of capitalism, a distorted and thinned-out version of Marx's purposeful activity or Nietzschean will. But as I have just been indicating, the repressions with regard to money—and, as I will argue following Freud and Norman O. Brown, the pathological nature of our culture's valuation of money—are far more powerful and persistent than parallel attitudes toward bodily love and its position in literature and life.

When money's power is acknowledged it is always criticized; almost as often, awareness of that power is repressed and denied, while in the fiction of at least the last 150 years, sexual and emotional repression is attacked. The two subject matters are complexly interrelated, and upon examination the money complex comes to be seen as guilt and renunciation, aliment becomes excrement, death in life. Thus what we find in love and money, those intertwined dualities at the heart of our literature, turns out to be life-affirming and its life-denying opposite, eros and thanatos.

From this perspective it is not hard to understand why our culture would both affirm and deny the power of money, why all literary assertions of that power are critical of what they assert. And when critics and theorists object so strenuously to Marxist assertions that money's power in literature points to its shaping power in our lives and that an urgent desire to illuminate such matters has been a crucial source of literary production, that objection is rooted in a desire to deny terrible truths and maintain the illusions that intellectual and artistic activity is free and independent of such forces.

i

Aristotle's denunciation of money's power is one of the first. In the *Politics* he contrasts what he calls "household management" wealth, in which effort and purpose is directed toward keeping self and family alive, fed and sheltered, with wealth as an acquisitive drive for accumulation of money for its own sake:

> There are two sorts of wealth-getting, as I have said; one is a part of household management, the other is retail trade: the former necessary and honorable, while that which consists in exchange is justly censured; for it is unnatural, and a mode by which men gain from one another. The most hated sort, and with the greatest reason, is usury, which makes a gain out of money itself, and not from the natural object of it. For money was intended to be used in exchange, but not to increase at interest. And this term interest, which means the birth of money from money, is applied to the breeding of money because the offspring resembles the parent. Wherefore of all modes of getting wealth this is the most unnatural.[7]

This text is the classical basis of the ethical critique of money's power, the source of the aristocratic aversion to vulgar trade and commerce, seen always as soiling and demeaning. And Aristotle's strong denunciation of usury (his sexual metaphor is of special interest in light of the view I will be arguing here) is at one with Christ's in the New Testament. The idea of money making money was emphatically denounced by Christ and the early Christians. But, of course, as money's power grew in medieval Europe, and as the secular power of the Church and its own wealth in money increased, Christ's prohibition was modified and usury was redefined, in a crucial and transparent change, as *excessive* interest.

The clear truth is that the power of money—usury, interest, money's ability to make money—lies at the very heart of the capitalist system. This truth violates all our moral standards, seems to make a mockery of all our ethics and to corrode with cynicism all other values. It is no wonder that we seek to deny this truth even as we recognize it.

Marx's observations on money are scattered throughout his works, as one would expect, but he is most explicit on the subject in "The Power of Money in Bourgeois Society," in the 1844 Manuscripts. His stress in that essay resembles that of Diderot in *Rameau's Nephew* in his insistence that when the cash nexus predominates and money is in the saddle, the rich man's ability to buy everything from horses to talent gives him a power which is nearly absolute, which renders nearly meaningless any other distinctions among men.⁸ At almost exactly the same time Balzac gave novelistic expression to that truth in these famous words:

> Everybody puts out his money at interest and turns it over as best he can. You're deluding yourself, dear angel, if you imagine that it's King Louis-Philippe that we're ruled by, and he has no illusions himself on that score. He knows, as we all do, that above the Charter there stands the holy, venerable, solid, the adored, gracious, beautiful, noble, ever young, almighty franc! Now, my fair angel, money calls for interest and is forever gathering it.⁹

The comparison and connection between royal power and that of money is important. It supports Jameson's insistence—basing his work on that of the *Tel Quel* group—on "the basic identity of value systems in general, whether on the economic, psychoanalytical, political, and linguistic levels." Further, he suggests, "the rich analogical content of various local studies of value—Marx's analysis of money and the commodity, Freud's of the libido, Nietzsche's of ethics, Derrida's of the word—is itself a sign of the hidden interrelationships of the categories which govern these various dimensions: gold, the phallus, the father or monarch or God, and the myth of the *parole pleine* or spoken word."¹⁰

Gold or money has a special status in that group; it is everywhere present but its power is always profoundly objectionable. The authority of a leader, the power of sexual energy or of the spoken word may or may not be illegitimate, objectionable. Such forces have their source in human beings, and can be alive and natural. But money's power over people seems the dominance of dead matter over life, and virtually all literary accounts of it are critical. Lionel Trilling faced the issue head on in *The Liberal Imagination*, where he argued that the novel arose in response to the increasing social dominance of money and that its great central themes of social aspiration and the problematic relationship between appearance and reality are rooted in money's power.¹¹ But our aversion to money's power is so strong and its implications as to the real nature of power in our society so discomforting that most critics seem intent on denying the shaping influence of money and social class in the realm of social life and culture. As Trilling puts it: "We believe that one of the unpleasant bedrock facts is social class, but we become extremely impatient if ever we are told that social class is indeed so real that it produces actual differences of personality."¹²

Now clearly, as my earlier quotation from Aristotle and the biblical "root of all evil" indicate, critical awareness of the power of money did not begin in the capitalist era. But it is equally clear that money is more centrally powerful in capitalism than ever before, that, in particular, the usurious function denounced by the early moralists is at the heart of that system, constitutes its basis, its real foundations. It is for that reason that it has been more difficult to recognize and denounce it than in a society in which it was more tangential to central economic and social activity. In the twentieth century, during which American and Western European money has ruled most of the world, our aversion to such truths and significances has become pathological. In his profound and far-reaching *Life Against Death*, Norman O. Brown devotes his longest chapter to a discussion of money's power and our need to deny it, the loathing it engenders. The chapter bears the title "Filthy Lucre."[13]

The connection between money and excrement established by the title is not new in the modern world either. Brown supplies many illustrations and examples of it, drawn from distant times and places. Hieronymus Bosch's famous fifteenth-century tryptich, "The Last Judgement," in the Prado clearly shows a naked man squatting and defecating gold coins. But it is in the capitalist era—first, in the work of Luther—that the connection becomes dominant in our culture and disastrous in the character structure to which it gives shape.

In addition to his literary and cultural anthropological sources, Brown bases his argument on Freudian theory and the clinical and analytical findings of depth psychology. It has of course been argued that the extrapolation from "sick" individuals to generalizations about a culture are without validity. But that argument ignores the real sources of what we call character or personality. As Christopher Lasch has argued recently, "the unconsious mind represents the modification of nature by culture, the imposition of civilization on instinct."[14] Further, says Lasch, we are correct in reading individual personality in terms of cultural forces since "every society reproduces its culture—its norms, its underlying assumptions, its modes of organizing experience—in the individual in the form of personality. . . . Each society tries to solve the universal crises of childhood . . . in its own way, and the manner in which it deals with these psychic events produces a characteristic form of psychological deformation, by means of which the individual reconciles himself to instinctual deprivation and submits to the requirements of social existence."[15]

I find Lasch's argument convincing and important. Many of Brown's basic premises violate common sense, but I believe that such aversion to the truths revealed by his analysis of our money culture has its source in the psychic conflicts he describes. We do not want to acknowledge what at some level we sense to be true—that money rules our lives, that money is excremental and hostile to life, and that money is important in fiction because it is at the source of the most important fictions in our lives. In fact, I would argue that all the attacks on naturalism in fiction by those who want to see "higher" things discussed (I am thinking especially of Tennyson's denunciation of "wallowing in the troughs of Zolaism") have their source not so much in the (related) fear of sexuality and general aversion to the body, but in a desire that the sources of the money/guilt/excrement complex remain repressed.

I have space here for only the barest outline of Brown's closely argued theory. The basic connection with which he begins is between money and quantifying rationality (p. 235). This is Blake's Urizenic, one-dimensional thought, a desire for possessive mastery over objects, over nature, "partial impulses in the human being (the human body) which in modern civilization have become tyrant organizers of the whole of human life" (p. 236). Money, he says, is for our culture the heir to religion, "an attempt to find God in things" (p. 240). Money's value is fetishistic, irrational, and sacred. Its intrinsic or use value is zero, and the hidden middle term connecting money to the sacred is power (p. 249). Privilege and prestige, says Brown, depend on renunciation, self-repression in the vast (unprivileged) majority. Thus it has resort to deception and enchantment to maintain itself (p. 252).

The basis for the equation of money and excrement is the former's "absolute worthlessness" (p. 254). What typifies modern capitalism is alienated, compulsive labor—not the production of necessities for "the Mouth," but superfluous production of fetishized commodities. The maintenance of such a situation is based on renunciation and sublimation—the rigidities of personality always associated by psychoanalysis with arrest at the anal stage of character development. This psychological principle of non-enjoyment is always part of compulsive, acquisitive enterprise. It is *not* natural or inevitable. As Brown puts it, "The modern psychology of possession is superimposed over a deeper psychology of giving, and is constructed, by the process of denial, out of its archaic opposite" (p. 264). This denial of the validity of the generous and life-affirming aspects of human nature divides us deeply, in ways which cripple us while they provide crucial support for the whole money complex.

"The whole money complex is rooted in guilt" argues Brown (p. 268).

That position is brilliantly supported by Nietzsche in his discussion of debt and payment, owe and ought, the cultural semantics of duty and obligation, which reduce a human being to his ability to repay a loan.[16] All currency, says Brown, is neurotic currency (p. 271). And our modern secular economy is an economy of guilt without redemption. As Luther argued, capitalism embodies what Christian mythology calls the Devil. And "the Devil (guilt) is lord of this world" (p.274).

Time, we are told, is money. And that linear, urgent preoccupation with time is, like money, neurotic and correlative with instinctual repression (p. 274). Obsessed with time, burdened with an urgent, guilty fear, we retreat into that greedy money/excrement complex, repressing our awarenesses of what we really need and desire and of the terrible cost of the renunciation we have accepted. To the extent that the money complex rules our culture and our society they are hostile to life and bent on self-destruction.

ii

Now, at some level we know all this is so. Were there no conflict involved in the renunciation required of us, if we really liked to live in or under excrement, we would not feel the inner longing and despair which social critics are always describing. And imaginative literature in our time is always responding to money power, either by flight, savage parody, or direct presentation and exposure. Modern literary response is more diverse than that in nineteenth-century realist fiction. In some modern novels the question is avoided entirely, as writers have sought to separate their work as much as possible from material reality, concentrating almost entirely on formal innovation, where the medium becomes the message. Elsewhere, as in the fictions of Kafka, the power of money remains crucially significant but is expressed obliquely and indirectly, in a form which combines allegory and fantasy or nightmare. But there are modernist works in which money is powerfully and immediately present. In such works the resonances of money/gold power are extended to other areas of human action and desire in ways that were still obscure in earlier realist fiction, though the sense of risk and fear all this raises is also strong. Thus the presentation of the deeper meanings of the money complex is often accompanied by a maze of modernist formal strategies which seem designed to distance and protect the author from responsibility for speaking such unpleasant truths.

In the three historical novels of E. L. Doctorow both the power of money and our reluctance to acknowledge it are centrally significant. His work does display the protective strategies to which I just referred, but the complex mixtures of distancing ironies and direct exposure he creates allow him to reveal the hidden sources of malaise in our culture more clearly than most modern writers. In particular, his historical fictions engage two areas of crucial significance: he makes our distortion and repression of awareness of the heart of the matter—what it means to live in a society where money's power is so complete—a central subject in his works, and he establishes the connections among money, excrement and power with savage irony.

Doctorow's approach to American history is radically ironic. In *Welcome to Hard Times* life on the barren northern prairies at the turn of the century is his subject and it is the traditional Western myths that he wishes to debunk. In *Ragtime* we are in the New York City of the first two decades of this century, and sentimental nostalgia and schoolbook histories of that era are the objects of his irony. *The Book of Daniel* seeks to expose the real source and nature of the Cold War and American life in the fifties and sixties. All in all, Doctorow's vision of twentieth-century American history is a terrible and negative one, which recalls Nietzsche's discussion of the historical sense in *The Use and Abuse of History*:

> The unrestrained historical sense, pushed to its logical extreme, uproots the future, because it destroys illusions and robs existing things of the only atmosphere in which they can live. Historical justice, even if practiced conscientiously, with a pure heart, is therefore a dreadful virtue, because it always undermines and ruins the living thing—its judgement always means annihilation. . . . For the historical audit brings so much to light which is false and absurd, violent and inhuman, that the condition of pious illusion falls to pieces.[17]

The illusions which Doctorow's historical vision seeks to uproot and destroy are those which would deny money's power or attempt to see that power as anything but cruel and destructive. Thus in *Ragtime* we get a strange mixture of lyrical evocations of a supposed "simpler era" with a bitter debunking of such illusions, illusions that would ignore the historical realities which decree that time is money. In the opening pages of exposition much of the novel's action is summarized, "giving it away" in a manner very like the placards held up at the beginning of each scene in Brecht's *Mother Courage and her Children*, for similar purposes of forcing ironic distance and thus forcing thought. The following excerpts illustrate the strange, flat and abrupt style—a disconcerting combination—and the debunking signification which is the aim of both style and subject matter:

> Patriotism was a reliable sentiment in the early 1900's. Teddy Roosevelt was President. . . . There seemed to be no entertainment that did not involve great swarms of people. Trains and steamers and trolleys moved them from one place to another. That was the style, that was the way people lived. Women were stouter then. They visited the fleet carrying white parasols. Everyone wore white in summer. Tennis racquets were hefty and the racquet faces elliptical. There was a lot of sexual fainting. There were no Negroes. There were no immigrants.[18]

Then, after many similar sentences but still in the three page opening paragraph—including this reference to Winslow Homer: "This was the time when Winslow Homer was doing his painting. A certain light was still available along the Eastern seaboard. Homer painted the light. It gave the sea a heavy dull menace and shone coldly on the rocks and shoals of the New England coast"—Evelyn Nesbit is introduced. She is the first of many actual historical personnages who have active roles in the novel:

> She had been a well-known artist's model at the age of fifteen. Her underclothes were white. Her husband habitually whipped her. She happened once to meet Emma Goldman, the revolutionary. Goldman lashed her with her tongue. Apparently there *were* Negroes. There *were* immigrants. (p. 5)

All is image and ersatz, disconnected. Doctorow is most directly satirizing the non-ironic presentation of the sort of text he is mocking in traditional schoolbook histories, wanting to destroy their easy and mystifying historical generalizations which prevent any accurate historical understanding. He seems almost to question the possibility of accurate linguistic, historical generalization, mocking our views of the past from art history to popular culture. But most centrally and challengingly, this passage, like the novel as a whole, tells us that our sentimental view of the past tells lies in seeking to conceal the realities of class and racial oppression and its support of the money complex; when we see "all people" dressed in white and amusing themselves we are actually seeing the past as if only the ruling class existed, specifically ignoring the very existence of the "Negroes and immigrants" who provide for its privileged position.

It is significant that Emma Goldman's radical anti-capitalism introduces the demystifying perspective in the novel (the role and fate of such radical vision is the main subject matter of *The Book of Daniel*). She insists on what has been the thesis of this essay—that our culture knows but does not want to know the obscene power of money, capital. Thus, key sections of the novel describe the terrible lives of immigrants in the Bowery, their famous textile strike in Lawrence, Massachusetts and its brutal repression. The main capitalists in the novel are Henry Ford and J. P. Morgan, representing industrial capital and finance capital respectively. In presenting Morgan Doctorow makes his most explicit statement on the power of money:

> Pierpont Morgan was that classic American hero, a man born to extreme wealth who by dint of hard work and ruthlessness multiplies the family fortune till it is out of sight. He controlled 741 directorships in 112 corporations. . . . Moving about in private railroad cars or yachts he crossed all borders and was at home everywhere in the world. He was a monarch of the invisible, transnational kingdom of capital whose sovereignty was everywhere granted. Commanding resources that beggared royal fortunes, he was a revolutionist who left to presidents and kings their territory while he took control of their railroads and shipping lines, banks and trust companies, industrial plants and public utilities. (pp. 158–59)

Again, the flat tone, the blunt, crude, simplified and summary approach. It is as if to break through the distortions and blindnesses it is necessary to imitate the comic book style which is usually the vehicle for the mystified vision he is attacking. But there is no denying the truth of his picture of Morgan. And the novel also clearly demonstrates the irrational, sacred power of money. Morgan's insane Orientalism represents such matters perfectly. Egyptian antiquity is Morgan's mode of attempting to establish belief in his own immortality. He plunders the graveyards of European, Classical and Egyptian cultures, illustrating Brown's view that the main architects of the money complex are "guilt, the aggressive fantasy of becoming father of oneself, and death anxiety or separation anxiety" (p. 290).

The second half of *Ragtime* centers around an allegorical contest between money power as symbolized by Morgan and those who suffer under it and may provide resistance to it, represented not by a historical character but by a fictional one, a black piano player named Coalhouse Walker. Like the money power he represents, and the electricity which will represent it in *The Book of Daniel*, Morgan is only rarely visibly present in this part of the novel, is out of the country during the final confrontation, during which Coalhouse and his gang occupy by force the huge, monumental Morgan library in New York City. Morgan's absence when his power is so present, exercised by surrogates, his employees and the police, represents fittingly that money power which it seems to be our culture's determination to deny all the more vehemently the more total and brutal it becomes.

Coalhouse, on the other hand, is very present indeed. He is a wonderful player of piano rags. ("Small clear chords hung in the air like flowers. The melodies were like bouquets. There seemed to be no other possibilities for life than those delineated by the music" [p. 183].) He speaks with grace and charm, and he regards the world with "large dark eyes so intense as to suggest they were about to cross" (p. 179). Most of all, he is a man of absolute devotion to principle; he defends his personal dignity fanatically, refusing to bend at all in the face of money power and racial prejudice.

All of this novel is a mixture of ironically employed clichés and stereotypes (parodying, as I have argued, our tendency to maintain our illusions by seeing the past that way) and startlingly original moments and movements which together attempt to alter and deepen our sense of real historical significances. And the incident which provokes the long confrontation with Morgan, state power, and all of white society is one of the strangest. Coalhouse has been driving out from Harlem to New Rochelle on Sundays, courting a woman who is already the mother of his child. His Model T is brightly polished, and he is dressed with style and flair. Some whites come to resent him as an uppity nigger, and on one occasion a group of volunteer firemen block the road in front of their station and demand a toll from Coalhouse. After a fruitless attempt to get help from a policeman, Coalhouse returns to his car. "It was spattered with mud. There was a six-inch tear in the custom panasote top. And deposited in the back seat was a mound of fresh human excrement" (p. 203).

Now I dare say there are very few other novels where excrement has such a place and significance. Coalhouse's rage is such that all the rest of his life is devoted to a violent quest for redress, a suicidal desperation, which does end in his death. And the startling presence of excrement in this situation points toward those life-denying and irrational roots and ramifications of the money power complex which are Brown's concern and the central subject of *Welcome to Hard Times*. Upon Coalhouse's occupation of the Morgan library, the police arrest Emma Goldman, for obvious if absurd reasons, and she speaks with reporters:

"... As an anarchist, I applaud his appropriation of the Morgan property. Mr. Morgan has done some appropriating of his own. At this the reporters shouted questions. Is he a follower of yours, Emma? Do you know him? Did you have anything to do with this? Goldman smiled and shook her head. The oppressor is wealth, my friends. Wealth is the oppressor. Coalhouse Walker did not need Red Emma to learn that. He needed only to suffer." (p. 322)

At the book's end, Mother's Younger Brother, a member of the narrator's family who has left his job in their fireworks factory to become ordnance man in Coalhouse's band, explains his actions to Father in words which connect the themes of the novel in a striking manner, words which again evoke Brown's view of capitalist power as excremental, unclean, life-denying, feeding on death:

> You are a complacent man with no thought of history. You pay your employees poorly and are insensitive to their needs. I see, Father said. The fact that you think of yourself as a gentleman in all your dealings is the simple self-delusion of all those who oppress humanity. . . . You have travelled everywhere and learned nothing, he said. You think it's a crime to come into this building belonging to another man and to threaten his property. In fact this is the nest of a vulture. The den of a jackal. (pp. 342–43)

iii

If *Ragtime* seeks to debunk the sentimental nostalgias of schoolbook American history, *Welcome to Hard Times* challenges those central Amercian myths of the frontier embodied in our traditional Westerns. Right from the start, the straight Westerns have evoked a counter-assertion. From the time of the earliest Westerns, other authors have felt the need to cast the myth in an ironic mode, to show the feet of clay, deflate idols and ideals which already in Stephen Crane's time were seen as false and mystifying, to suggest the inadequacy of these myths in the face of the actual modern world. In such books false gods are revealed; a pessimistic "realism" constantly reveals new ways in which the traditional version rests on values, assumptions, views of reality which are unreal, false, insubstantial— either as a result of deliberate distortion and deception or of naive wishful thinking, the repressive embarrassment with which I began this essay.

I would argue that from Crane's "Blue Hotel" to Doctorow's *Welcome to Hard Times*, the central concern has been to expose the predominance of money, greed and force on the frontier, to reveal the extent to which the spirit and practice of capitalism, of hucksterism and exploitation, underlie and belie the more noble myths of conflict on the frontier. Crane in 1900 and Doctorow in 1975 both seek to expose the inadequacy and insanity of the ideology of individualism, both as an account of the experience of the West and as an answer to our problems. These writers use epic or mythic elements and conventions to teach us the inner truths of our national traditions, truths concealed rather than revealed by the traditional Western. And the myth which such authors propose as a substitute for the one they are debunking points to a world where the isolated individual—such a positive figure in the familiar Western—is in a hopeless situation, with no real community, no stay against the storm.

In Crane's story the mystifying myths of manly combat in the American west blind the alien Swede to the realities of Scully the hotel keeper's boosterism and hucksterism and to the economic interests which are of real concern to the good citizens of the tavern where he meets his death, with the price he paid for his last drink still showing on the cash register. In Doctorow's reworking of our national mythos of the frontier, a tiny town on the barren flats of the Dakota territory around the time of Crane and of *Ragtime* is the scene of a violent cycle of death and destruction, commercial enterprise, more death and destruction. In *Hard Times* the spirit of the frontier is the sadism of the death instinct, expressed both in arbitrary machismo violence and the alienating manipulations of commercial self-interest.

The world Doctorow shows us is a place where what is needed is real community, but life in *Hard Times* offers only the illusion, the appearance of community; the only real ties among humans there are those of the cash nexus. Such an assemblage—like the strivings of traditional will and virtue—proves terribly inadequate in the face of the related threats of sadistic violence and economic ruin.

Welcome to Hard Times tells the story of two and a half years in the life of its tiny town. It begins with the destruction of the town and the murder of five of its nine citizens by an archetypal "mysterious stranger" of the first order, a man always refered to as "the Bad Man from Bodie."[19] The town is painfully rebuilt from its ashes (from lumber salvaged from nearby "dead towns"), and grows a little as a result of what turn out to be false hopes of economic fortune. The book ends with a scene of complete anarchy and violence, as the Eastern banks pull out their money and the Bad Man from Bodie returns and lays waste once again to the town. Everyone either flees or dies, and the deserted town is left to the buzzards feeding on the corpses, empty, except for one crazy woman and the slowly dying narrator.

There is no escaping this novel's savage debunking of any and all innocent pastoral myths of life on the frontier. It is of course true that money and violence are very common elements in the traditional Western, but there their effect is softened and mystified so that they appear as of only secondary significance, their meaning confined to the "test" they provide to the rugged individual who is the real subject of the tale. In *Hard Times* individualist responses to the catastrophic events are completely inadequate.

The story is told in the first person by a man named Blue, the Mayor of the town, his title having come to him not from an election but from his habit of writing things down, of keeping records, and because he is the prime mover in trying to make a town of that barren place. He writes his account of the town's history in three of the ledger books which have been provided him in his capacity as agent for the stage-coach company, ledgers where he has also recorded the business transactions which have been the only life of the town. As he composes his narrative of the town's terrible history he looks at the earlier entries and remarks that "the pages are full of dealings, of claims and ownings."[20] Thus the centrality of profit-loss economics in Doctorow's account of the West is always being suggested by what is posited of the pages themselves, those ledgers, and the accompanying assumption of the primacy of "the bottom line."

The mystifications of the familiar Western mode form a central subject of Blue's narrative. Near the end he tells us: "Like the West, like my life: the color dazzles us, but when it's too late we see what a fraud it is" (p. 186). And twice he evokes the egalitarian, libertarian aspect of the traditional myth of the West as the lie that brought him and the others out from the East—the idea that out there "if you're half a man you can make your life without too much trouble" (p. 28).

But not only the mystifications of such myths are brought under Blue's critical scrutiny. His narration is highly self-conscious and self-critical, repeatedly calling into question the very possibility of truth in this or any other narrative. Again and again, more frequently as the book progresses, he interrupts the story to repeat his purpose: "to tell the truth about what happened" or "to tell how things were," but always to express his feeling that he has failed to do so, that he can't get it right. He has a radical distrust of language itself—"as if some marks in a book could control things" (p. 187). In separate passages near the end of the novel he wonders, "Does the truth come out in such scrawls, so bound by my limits?" (p. 213), and expresses his fear that his narrative has not shown "the terrible arrangement of our lives" (p. 203).

That radical distrust of language is of course a particularly modern theme, and for Doctorow it is intimately connected to his central concern, the terrible helplessness in a world where humans are connected only by money (the "terrible arrangement" in the phrase I just quoted). It is said that money talks, but Bob Dylan tells us that that isn't true, that "Money doesn't talk, it swears" ("It's Alright Ma, I'm Only Bleeding"). In a world where only economic relations really matter, as social critics since the Enlightenment have been telling us, all other values are eroded and distorted, and the real, viable connections of community will not be present. For language not to be deceptive and obscuring, some sort of basis for trust must exist. If the "circuit of speech" is only a vehicle for cynical self-interest, such trust is continually being destroyed. Language does not connect, it deceives, it controls, it manipulates. In a sense it can be said that real speech ceases to exist. This disintegration or superfluity of language is brilliantly symbolized by Doctorow in the Bad Man from Bodie, who never speaks. Twice he destroys the town, smiling all the while as he rapes and murders, burns and destroys. But we never hear him speak a word (some may remember Aldo Ray's great, silent, smiling, evil presence in the movie version). So language is impotent or misleading in this novel. Only violence and money communicate, and what they say *is* more swearing than talking.

What Doctorow seeks to show in this novel is a pattern of economic and psychological relationships which are concealed rather than revealed by the traditional accounts of the Western experience, where capitalism's relationships are the basis for an existence and a culture which make a mockery of traditional values and norms of conduct, of the liberal vision of individual purpose or quest. He makes his view the basis for a new de-mystified myth, a myth of sleazy self-interest, fear, and macho violence. Zar, the Russian whore master, tells Blue, "Frand . . . I come West to farm . . . but soon I learn, I see . . . farmers starve . . . only people who sell farmers their land, their seed, their tools . . . only these people are rich. And that is the way with everything" (pp. 63–64). And in fact the town is entirely parasitical; it has no agriculture, no industry. Its residents sell sex, booze and general merchandise to miners who are working a company lode in the nearby hills. Blue is willing to appeal to commercial hopes and motives in his desperate desire to get people to live in town, but he is all too aware that this accumulation of jealous, selfish, frightened men forms no community. Molly, the former prostitute who was terribly treated by the Bad Man from Bodie on his first visit and now lives only on her desire for revenge, tells Blue that his zeal for settlers is only a pathetic desire to be part of a herd. And, in fact, it is of that that Blue dreams: "I dreamed the Man from Bodie was driving a herd across some badland: and riding each head was a wolf or some buzzard with its claws planted. I was in the Middle, running with the rest, and I couldn't shake free of the claws" (p. 44). A herd and not a community, what Sartre calls seriality, the illusion or substitute for community in our society, where isolated monads are connected only by the alienating ties and fetters of ownership and marketplace.

A striking feature of this novel is the repeated allusion to excrement. On the first page we are told that the wagon trains on the horizon left "a long dust turd lying on the rim of the earth." On the third page one of the Bad Man's first victims ends up on his knees in a fresh pile of manure. There are many other examples. Molly frequently refers contemptuously to the men of the town as "filth" or "shit." Now, on one level such language and such themes have the effect of putting an ironic distance between Doctorow's narrative and the traditional "clean" Western pastoral. But I think the shit is there for a deeper reason, to help embody a vision which ties together the themes of the book, quite deliberately pointing to the ideas suggested by Norman O. Brown. "Money is condensed wealth," Brown says; "condensed wealth is condensed guilt. But guilt is essentially unclean. 'Monks eat the world's excrement, that is to say sins,' says Rabelais" (p. 266). Like Brown, Doctorow suggests that compulsive, competitive money making, the commercial spirit of capitalism, is pathological and destructive, part of a structure of repressed, sublimated and distorted eros which manifests itself as secret, compulsive sexuality, guilt and a connected set of moral and financial debts and obligations, sadism and masculine violence—Thanatos, the death instinct.

"Until the advent of psychoanalysis and its doctrine of the anal character of money," says Brown, "the profoundest insights into the nature of the money complex had to be expressed through the medium of myth—in modern times, the myth of the Devil" (p. 301). In Doctorow's myth the Devil is the Bad Man from Bodie. He brings fire and death to the town; Blue tells us that the embers glowing on the ground after the Bad Man has gone were "like peep holes to hell" (p. 31). And it is this malignant figure which links money and excrement, violent sex and violent death, that Doctorow sees as the embodiment of the nightmare actualities which are concealed or denied by the traditional Western. For Doctorow as for Brown, prudential calculation, the hoarding of wealth, excrement, and violence, these are the pathological traits characteristic of Western society. When the bankers from the East pull their money out of the mine, killing the town, Blue calls them "Those white-faced, black-derbied Eastern sons of Hell!" (p. 192), pulling together the threads, establishing the connections between the Bad Man's violence and the money relations which have sickened the life of the town.

What the town needs against the arbitrary cruelty, the absolute amorality and cynicism represented by the Bad Man from Bodie, would be some real ties among its inhabitants, ties of love and obligation which could fuel some courageous, intelligent opposition. And during the period of the town's growth, when the possibility of increased Eastern banking investment in the mines seemed to promise prosperity, Blue even dares to articulate such hopes, that they'd be ready if the Bad Man came back. Molly derides his hopes: "Oh Jesus God, spare me from this man, this talker" (p. 152). She tells him that none of its residents care about the town, that they're all only in it for the money. He replies with the hope that "if business is good" that won't matter.

But when the hopes disappear, when the people flee the town and the Bad Man returns, Blue realizes that she was right, that his visions of brotherhood and sharing in such a situation were ridiculous, absurd. In the final holocaust, Molly and the Bad Man both die, and Blue is mortally wounded. Death, destruction, rotting corpses in the street are the only fruits borne by this awful narrative.

iv

In *The Book of Daniel* Doctorow's concern is with two moments from much more recent history than his turn of the century narratives, the Cold War of the early fifties and the anti-Viet Nam war period of the late sixties. He concentrates in that novel on the repressive force of money power embodied both in the state and the "private" sector, and on the dangers to those who oppose that power, who seek to expose the myths and illusions which allow it to maintain its power. As Doctorow puts it, to see that money complex for what it really is is to "make the connections," connections we are not supposed to acknowledge, like that between money and excrement. He even tells us that liberalism is "the failure to make connections. The failure to make connections is complicity."[21]

The radical, on the other hand, does make the connections, but he does so at considerable risk. In seeing what he is not supposed to see and saying what he is not supposed to say, the radical writer or intellectual or political activist becomes, in a phrase repeated again and again in the novel, "a criminal of perception" (pp. 41, 44, 87, 291). The most explicit statement on the subject is this one:

> I have an idea for an article. If I write it maybe I can sell it and see my name in print. The idea is the dynamics of radical thinking. With each cycle of radical thought there is a stage of genuine creative excitement during which the connections are made. The radical discovers connections between available data and the root responsibility. Finally he connects everything. At this point he loses his following. It is not that he has incorrectly connected anything, it is that he has connected everything. Nothing is left outside the connections. At this point society becomes bored with the radical. Fully connected in his characterization it has achieved the counterinsurgent rationale that allows it to destroy him. The radical is given the occasion for one last discovery—the connection between society and his death. After the radical is dead his early music haunts his persecutors. And the liberals use this to achieve power. (pp. 155–56)

Like the "atom bomb spies," Julius and Ethel Rosenberg, who in the novel are the Isaacsons, the narrator's parents, those who make the connections and are motivated thereby to oppose the money complex and seek to change it face the real possibility of being destroyed by it. The central metaphor in the novel for both those connections and the hidden power of capital, invisible but deadly, absent when present, is electricity.

Electricity works perfectly as a central metaphorical device in this novel. It represents the hidden, potentially deadly power of those forces which connect all aspects of our lives. The representative power of modern civilization, it pervades our lives, participates in virtually all aspects of production, shapes both the commodities and the artificial appetites that will seek out those products in impossible hopes for fulfillment and meaning. It carries the television messages which, as McLuhan and others have told us, so dominate our consciousness that "the medium is the message." Electricity connects us all into what Buckminster Fuller sees positively as "the global village." But to those who see the real motive force of this society to be maximizing profit, expanding the capital of those in power, the network into which electricity connects us all is likely to appear more like a concentration camp than a village.

Electricity also powers Disneyland, where one of the novel's final scenes is enacted. Electricity allows the Disney conglomerate to take whatever it wants from our literary culture—*Alice in Wonderland, Snow White, Huckleberry Finn*, etc.—and shape it to its ends. "Most of them have passed through a previous process of film or animation and are made to recall the preemptive power of the Disney organization with regard to Western culture" (p. 303). Few children, says Doctorow, who ride in the Mad Hatter's Teacup will have read *Alice*, and thus they will know it only through the Disney film, if at all. "And that suggests a separation of at least two ontological degrees between the Disneyland customer and the cultural artifacts he is presumed upon to treasure in his visit. . . . And even to an adult who dimly remembers reading the original *Alice*, and whose complicated response to this powerfully symbolic work has long since been incorporated into the psychic constructs of his life, what is being offered does not suggest the resonances of the original work, but is only a sentimental compression of something that is already a lie" (p. 304).

Daniel draws out the specific political implications of his view of Disneyland like this: "What Disneyland proposes is a technique of abbreviated shorthand culture for the masses, a mindless thrill, like an electric shock, that insists at the same time on the recipient's rich psychic relation to his country's history and language and literature. In a forthcoming time of highly governed masses in an overpopulated world, this technique may be extremely useful both as a substitute for education and, eventually, for experience" (p. 305). Thus Disneyland is shown as a manifestation of the inter-connected nature of mass cultural, political, technological and economic forces, and as a tool whereby actual political-private relationships are at once concealed and debased. Mindless, manipulative spectacle is substituted for the sort of experience which might satisfy real needs and lead to an awareness of the existence and significance of mediating connections through the political to the money complex on the part of so many citizens now anesthetized by the Disneyland, McDonald's, Howard Johnson's world.

"And behold, it came to pass, just the kind of world we said it was" (p. 254). Thus ends Doctorow's *raga* history of the Cold War. And that points to the importance of *The Book of Daniel*. Like his fictions of our more distant past, this novel directs us back toward the awarenesses of the connections between the public and private, political and personal I discussed earlier, relations for so long obscured rather than illuminated by American fiction, at least as it is conventionally discussed. Doctorow considers and represents the many ways we have been shaped by the powerful forces which direct modern life. He reveals as well those cultural forces which have obscured and mystified the nature and power of those shaping forces.

In all of his historical fiction, Doctorow uses irony to debunk the mystifications which support the illusions which keep us from facing the truths of the money complex. Those truths have been articulated by thinkers from Aristotle and Christ to Freud and Brown. But much of our culture has sought to deny their validity or significance, has refused to recognize the terrible and total power of money in our lives and its disastrous effects. Yet poets like Blake and Wordsworth raised their voices against money and its calculating, repressive culture, and such voices cannot be entirely stilled. The dominance of money *is* wrong, dirty. It poisons the well springs of life. But barring some unthinkable "final solution" the life force will resist, Eros will fight back against Thanatos, and it will be our poets and novelists who give voice to that vision.

NOTES

1. Karl Marx, "Preface" to *A Contribution to the Critique of Political Economy*, *The Marx-Engels Reader*, ed. Robert C. Tucker, second edition (New York: Norton, 1978), p. 184.
2. Fredric Jameson, *The Prison-House of Language* (Princeton: Princeton University Press, 1972), p. 184.
3. *Ibid.*
4. For a fine recent examination and defense of this position see Fredric Jameson, "Marxism and Historicism," *New Literary History*, 9 (1979), 41–73, esp. pp. 67–72.
5. Raymond Williams, *The Country and the City* (London: Oxford University Press, 1973), pp. 51–54.
6. Williams, pp. 113–17, 167–69.
7. Aristotle, *Politics*, trans. Benjamin Jowett (New York: Modern Library, 1943), p. 71.
8. Karl Marx, "The Power of Money in Bourgeois Society," Tucker, pp. 101–05.
9. Honore de Balzac, *Cousin Bette*, trans. Marion Ayton Crawford (London: Penguin, 1965), p. 305.
10. Jameson, *Prison-House*, pp. 180–81.
11. Lionel Trilling, "Manners, Morals and the Novel," "Art and Fortune," in *The Liberal Imagination* (New York: Doubleday, 1953), pp. 200–15, 245–67.

12. Trilling, p. 209. This repression of awareness, this refusal to acknowledge what at some level we know, is central to what Marxists call reification or false consciousness. Fredric Jameson speaks to the question in "Reification and Utopia in Mass Culture," *Social Text*, 1 (Winter, 1979), where he argues that the aestheticism and withdrawal of literature professors has a symbolic content and expresses "(generally unconsciously) the anxiety aroused by market competition and the repudiation of the primacy of business pursuits and business values: these are then, to be sure, as thoroughly repressed from academic formalism as culture is from the work of the sociologists of manipulation, a repression which goes a long way towards accounting for the resistance and defensiveness of contemporary literary study towards anything which smacks of the painful reintroduction of just that 'real life'—the socio-economic, the historical context—which it was the function of the aesthetic vocation to deny or to mask out in the first place" (p. 139).

13. Norman O. Brown, *Life Against Death: The Psychoanalytical Meaning of History* (New York: Vintage Books, 1959), pp. 234–304. All subsequent references are to this edition and will be indicated parenthetically in the text.

14. Christopher Lasch, *The Culture of Narcissism: American Life in an Age of Diminishing Expectations* (New York: Warner Books, 1979), p. 77.

15. *Ibid.*, p. 76.

16. Nietzsche, *The Geneology of Morals*, in *Basic Writings of Nietzsche*, trans. and ed. Walter Kaufmann (New York: Modern Library, 1968), pp. 499–508.

17. Nietzsche, *The Use and Abuse of History*, trans. Adrian Collins (Indianapolis: Library of Liberal Arts, 1977), p. 42.

18. E. L. Doctorow, *Ragtime* (New York: Bantam, 1975), pp. 3–5. All subsequent references are to this edition and will be indicated parenthetically in the text.

19. For an illuminating discussion of the power and prevalence of this trope in American literature, see Roy Male, *Enter, Mysterious Stranger* (Norman: Univ. of Oklahoma Press, 1979).

20. E. L. Doctorow, *Welcome to Hard Times* (New York: Bantam, 1976), p. 134. All subsequent references are to this edition and will be indicated parenthetically in the text.

21. E. L. Doctorow, *The Book of Daniel* (New York: Signet, 1971), p. 243. Subsequent references are to this edition and will be indicated parenthetically in the text.

Contra Naturam?:
Usury in William Gaddis's *JR*

Steven Weisenburger
University of Kentucky

William Gaddis is the author of two Big Books. By this designation I mean that *The Recognitions* (1955) and *JR* (1975) stand in a brotherly relation to *Moby-Dick*, *Ulysses*, *The Sot-Weed Factor*, and *Gravity's Rainbow*. They tend to put us off by their sheer bulk, five hundred pages long at the least, like tirelessly constructed monuments to knowledge and wit. We finish reading one and echo Samuel Johnson on *Paradise Lost*: "None ever wished it any longer than it is." Yet the Big Book is demonstrably the most important (and ironic) kind being written in America, and Gaddis's two are masterful examples of the form. Strange to say, then, that with the exception of a National Book Award for his second novel, Gaddis's writing receives little recognition and scarcely any critical discussion. Five years after its publication, *JR*, a brilliantly funny and accessible book, stands unnoticed.[1]

This is not the place for a full-length consideration of Big Books, needful as that is, but a few remarks on the form will help preface my discussion of *JR*.[2] First, Big Books concern themselves with Man's attempted mastery of Nature, but the frame for Man's struggle is Commerce: whaling, travelling salesmanship, colonizing Maryland, building rockets. This is particularly so in American varieties of the form, whose authors are still laying siege against our old Whiggish optimism about making and marketing commodities. Like Melville, they start to exclaim "Ah Bartleby! Ah humanity!", then they set to work on a book Big enough to properly do it.

Narrative tension in a Big Book arises when the claims of imaginative freedom, usually in the person of an artist, are made to correlate with natural necessity, that is, Commerce as the need of people to be useful by turning Nature's riches into gain. Yet the needs of Commerce and those of Art never square with each other, and so the artist discovers his eternally painful relationship with Nature—not in mastery but in estrangement. He may even display his estrangement like a badge, as in *Humboldt's Gift*, where Citrine's hammered-in Mercedes-Benz becomes just such a figure. And at the end, the revelation of the artist's struggle does make identities clear: *this* is the right use of imagination, we say at the conclusion; or, this is the true artist and here the test of genuine art. Thus, as *Gravity's Rainbow* concludes Pynchon is affirming the imaginative spark—compassion—that links characters together and lifts them above the traps of technology and into "systems of caring." And in *The Octopus*, Norris adopts the long view on Preston's failed battle against the railroaders: "Falseness dies," he writes in the last paragraph. Commerce, as a degenerative system of exchange, always takes this kind of moral drubbing at the end of the Big Book. In the final scenes of Robert Coover's *The Public Burning* it resembles nothing less than a sideshow metastasized into banal, murderous demagoguery. And I think that, despite all the talk about where to "place" it, *The Executioner's Song* precisely fits this description. In Norman Mailer's hands Gary Gilmore becomes a type of the artist (he was a painter) who cannot fit, shoplifts for the heck of it, commits senseless murder, but still *articulates* his own death. That is why Mailer has to include his Afterword; he has to indicate that his book, unlike what all the other hacks might have done with a congeries of tapes and letters, is the true artistic rendering of Gilmore's story.

This is the mode Gaddis works in, and I suspect we have only begun to appreciate its value. I intend chiefly to open several lines of approach to a fine novel that we have neglected, yet I also hope the following discussion will suggest lines of inquiry into Big Books as a genre. The questions after all are fascinating: What are the structural resources of storytelling in a Post-industrial leviathan such as America? Where *do* artists fit in, if anywhere? In what ways do we confuse Art and Money?

Depreciation is the principal topic of Gaddis's *JR*. In this novel the desire for commercial and transcendental wealth—for money and artworks—brings into play two related difficulties: the apparent similarity (even identity) of money and language, and the degeneration of monetary and artistic wealth inside a system based on principles of usury. To Gaddis, when money talks, things fall apart. Using money depreciates real wealth and using language depreciates meaning, thus nullifying Art. Edward Bast, the artist-figure in *JR*, finds himself struggling to be free of the institutional usury that wastes his creative vitality, but his crucial discovery is that usury itself is the state of Nature. Usury is not *contra naturam*, as we may have thought from reading *The Merchant of Venice* or Ezra Pound's *Cantos*. No, it partakes of Nature's vast commerce, for even molecules exchange particles and yield up energy (interest) during the transaction. Pound's condemnations in Canto 45 ("with usura the line grows thick"; it is "CONTRA NATURAM") reveal a limitation to Bast because he sees it is everything outside Art, everything in usurious Nature, that is inexorably diminishing in worth.

More accurately, not Bast but the structural patterning of *JR* as a Big Book makes these discoveries for us. At first glance this seems absurd, for the writing in *JR* is utterly seamless, without any familiar narrative divisions. Spatio-temporal transitions occur without warning, often in the midst of sentences. That is, when characters speak sentences. Owing to the flux of events they rarely surpass the phrase level of utterance, and Gaddis segues one voice into another with no identifying marks, so that *JR* reads like an extended transcription of tape-recorded noise. One character repeats a bit of financial jargon, "accelerated depreciation," that aptly describes the state of language in this novel, where everyone seems hell-bent on voicing cliché, tautology, cant, obscenity, nonsense.

Yet standing against this chaos of narration are remarkable intricacies of reference and structure. I want to trace three fields of reference basic to *JR*, these being Wagner's *Ring*, Empedocles's cosmology, and entropy theory. Taken together they represent synecdochically the branches of human knowledge—in art, philosophy, and natural philosophy—that Gaddis relates to his central theme of depreciation or usury. These references mediate our reading of the structural oppositions on which the novel depends. They indicate (on the one hand) a commercial Nature run amok with greed, strife and chaos, and (on the other) the struggles of the artist to create inherently useless and self-sufficient works. As I have indicated, this is the crucial test of a Big Book, and Gaddis shapes the triumph of his protagonist, Edward Bast, into the touchstone with which we may tell the truth of human motives and the genuineness of Art.

What Homer's *Odyssey* is to Joyce's *Ulysses*, Richard Wagner's *Der Ring des Nibelungen* is to *JR*. The *Ring* cycle serves as mythic sub-text to the fictional plot, and Gaddis introduces the parallels between them early in the book. The opening scene involving Bast's great aunts abruptly shifts to a Brooklyn school where we meet the main characters.[3] These include Jack Gibbs, seen lecturing on information theory and the Second Law of

Thermodynamics to eighth-grade students who can't even spell the word "e-n-t-r-o-p-y," as well as Edward Bast, working as a composer-in-residence at the school, seen attempting to direct a class of sixth graders in "The Rhinegold." One of Bast's pupils is J. R. Vansant, who first appears in a glass phone booth, "motionless but for fragmenting finger and opposable thumb opening, closing, the worn snap of an old change purse" (p. 31). He is a runny-nosed, disheveled kid obsessed with the hollow promises of mail-order fortunes, a boy whom the kindly describe as someone hungering and desolate for success and the cynical as someone "about as touching as a bull shark" (p. 246). In the school's presentation of "The Rhinegold," and in the novel, JR plays Alberich, the grotesque, gnomish creature who renounces love for the power to enslave men by possessing the Nibelung Ring. As in the operas, Gaddis holds up love as the source of all beneficent creativity, and when JR shouts his lines in rehearsal—"Hark floods! Love I renounce forever!" (p. 36)—Gaddis signals the genesis of what will become, in the phenomenally short span of just three months, the "JR Family of Companies," an international consortium of cut-throat business interests capable of disrupting the life of every character in the novel. Read as a fable of business, *JR* (like the *Ring*) represents the origins of American commerce as a little monster, Primal Greed, living inside all of us.

References to Wagner are scattered thoughout the first scenes of *JR*, but they all center on the depletion of love as a twilight age in Nature. Shortly after his renunciation of love, JR attends Mrs. Joubert's field trip to the Wall Street skyscraper Valhalla where a confrontation with the gods of finance ensues. In Crawley, a stock-broker who hunts wild pigs "with lances" (p. 88), he meets one of Wotan's spearmen. But it is at best a faltering Valhalla: a stockholder's suit is pending against the Diamond Cable branch of the business, which the class buys a share of; and "Monty" Moncrief (they all have redundant names, like "Dave" Davidoff) rushes about battling corporate "brush fires." The *Götterdammerung* cannot be far off. Amy Joubert, the daughter of Governor Cates (Wotan in this Valhalla), seems to sense an impending collapse. As Brunnhilde, she represents the gods' estrangement from their own better selves, for she is loving, dignified, aloof and sensitive, but the Valhallans mock her for all that and press her into business deals designed to salvage the family wealth.

JR moves through this faltering Valhalla and sees it as a fabulous game, as though Gaddis meant for us to take Wagner literally when he wrote of the Rhinegold that it is "worthless, except when you play."[4] Moncrief explains to him the crass objectives to this financial game— "I'd just say boys and girls, as long as you're in the game you may as well play to win" (p. 107)—which gives JR the idea that anything goes so long as you can bend a rule to cover yourself. He will be repeating Moncrief's dictum until the novel's end. He also learns a pair of simple rules from Amy's father: "buy for credit sell for cash," Cates tells him in the executive toilet; the second rule is, the "money is credit" that makes more gain possible (pp. 108–09). It is a vicious, usurious circle, and yet precisely that set of rules confers on JR a Ring-like power over mankind. His empire begins from ads in mail-order catalogues. Clipping coupons and operating from the school phone booth, he works a deal to buy four and a half million surplus picnic forks from the United States Air Force, on credit, and sell them to the Army at a wild profit. Business booms. JR acquires bankrupt companies, empty mining claims, an entire New England mill town full of pensioned-off employees, quantities of pork bellies, flawed Chinese sweaters, plastic flowers, an unfinished ship hull as a tax write off, a chain of nursing homes that feed business to another chain of funeral parlors, the Bast family company that makes piano rolls, and a subsidiary of it that manufactures sheep-gut condoms. The JR Corp. is built up from the incomplete, the obsolete, the fruitless, the dead.

The risible part of it is that JR succeeds because he mimics the gods of Commerce so well, following the clichéd laws of their game to the letter. The irony is, like Alberich, he becomes a joke in Valhalla. Looking over a class picture taken when Mrs. Joubert's class visited Diamond Cable, Davidoff points to JR and laughs: "look at this one, down in front here holding up the stock certificate," he says, "ever see so much greed confined in one small face?" (p. 461). What they don't know, by the mid-point in the story, is that they are now on the job for JR, who whips them to work across the invisible distances of telephone connections, like Alberich flogging his Nibelungs to work in the mines. They simply know him as "The Boss," and grant that "he does the grunting and we do the work" (p. 526). By the end, JR has almost brought down Valhalla itself, a fact that he takes delight in when they begin to make the *Wall Street Journal*: "JR Corp. appears threatened by a credit squeeze whose dramatic repercussions could be felt throughout the corporate world" (pp. 649–50). Thus, the fearful thing is that the monster in JR is capable of witlessly bringing down the world.

Against all his artistic principles, Bast allows JR to blandish him until there is no choice but to serve the company that can't even spell his name properly (it comes out "Edwerd" on Bast's business cards). The business grows on Bast like a cancer. He begins to sound more and more like JR when he talks, and throughout Bast's frenzied work JR keeps assuring him that it is all designed to give him money so he will have freedom to do his artwork. Bast finally rejects their corporate success in a climactic scene when, his voice nearly gone from pneumonia, he manages to scream at JR: "you ruin everything you touch . . . why not smash everything? . . . the JR Family of Companies bringing America its full share of holy shit! . . . you can't get up to their level so you drag them down to yours" (pp. 658–59). In the end, the JR Corporation symbolizes everything wasteful and excremental transformed through Commerce into a mockery of the sacred. And while Bast eventually frees himself to go his own artistic way there is the troubling fact that JR, stripped of his empire by the I.R.S. and the S.E.C., will doubtless rise again like Hagen the son of Alberich. When last we hear him on the telephone, JR excitedly spells out his plans for a lecture tour of college campuses. Thus we finish *JR* with a sense of foreboding. This Alberich, whom Wagner described as a "darksome foe of love," only needs maturity to bring on the final *Götterdammerung*.

The technique of Gaddis's allusions to Alberich can be formulated in this way: he begins with a constituting scene, the school children's rehearsal of "The Rhinegold," then follows with less explicit references that nevertheless map the overall *Ring* myth onto JR's progress. This means that J. R. Vansant, like Alberich, will disappear from the action for lengthy periods when our attention shifts to Gaddis's mock-hero, Bast.

And if JR represents a composite of Wagner's Alberich/Hagen characters, then Bast embodies both the Siegmund and Siegfried characters from the *Ring*. Once more Gaddis introduces these parallels with a constituting scene, which occurs when Bast and his step-sister, Stella Angel, attempt intercourse in the upstairs room of a tower behind the Bast home. We have thus moved further into the *Ring* cycle, for countless details link Bast and Stella to Siegmund and Sieglinda in Act One of "The Valkyrie": claps of thunder overhead as they fall onto the bed, flashes of lightning when Bast enters her, the high tower recalling Hunding's mountaintop retreat, and Bast carrying for years in his memory the image of Stella swimming naked, like Siegmund, who claims that Sieglinda is the "picture long hid in my heart."[5] These details all stem from Wagner, but Gaddis includes a crucial departure from the opera. Bast's spur-of-the-moment tryst with Stella ends in *coitus interruptus* when her dim-witted husband, Norman, stumbles into the tower. ("Sorry, it's a hell of a way to meet you," he says on page 140, ignorant of what's been going on upstairs.) There is a deeper irony, too, in the fact that while Bast's passions are serendipitous and purely romantic, Stella has engineered the seduction to obtain certain legal papers from her half-brother. Nevertheless, Bast thinks he has discovered in their stormy tryst a recognition of the *Ring* myth. He sits down at his piano and begins pounding out "the Ring motif" and singing Sieglinda's lines from the libretto (p. 142). Stella ought to get the gist of Bast's wild behavior because she has been reading a book called *Wagner: Man and Artist*, yet she is blinded from this artistic connection by her greed. And Bast is simply too naive at this point in the novel to question Stella's cold-hearted motives. Still, while Bast may not be a stencil of Siegmund here, the offspring of their frustrated coupling will be a new Bast who makes his way into the greedy world, literally parentless (as we will see), like Siegfried.

After this scene, the allusions to the operas become more generalized, as Bast drifts into the maelstrom of the JR Corporation, becomes its chief agent, even scores a fortune for JR while his musical compositions lie uncompleted. Gaddis suggests that Bast's sojourn inside the monolith of Commerce parallels Siegfried's battle with Fafner, from whom he may win the power of the Rhinegold. Bast also defeats a dragon, insofar as he pulls off a series of coups for JR, and like his Wagnerian counterpart the victory sets his blood aflame. Siegfried's amazed cry—"Rushing flows my feverish blood!"—becomes in Bast a literal fever brought on by exhaustion and pneumonia. The ills of capitalism injure him just as they finally stab Siegfried in the back.

Sick with pneumonia, Bast burns with a fever like Siegfried's corpse flaming on its funeral pyre in "The Twilight of the Gods." This, coupled with the increasing frequency of Jack Gibbs God-damning everything in the last sections of the novel, seems to anticipate a *Götterdammerung* very close indeed to Wagner's tragic ending. Moreover, Governor Cates (Wotan) has also been brought low by the press of business. As the novel closes he is admitted into the same hospital room Bast is preparing to leave for repair work on his artificial heart. (Surely there is a metaphor in that.) But here occurs another important departure from the *Ring* myth, for Gaddis's Siegfried does not die. When Bast recovers he redeems not only his health but his Art, a triumph Gaddis figures in Bast's retrieving the musical scores he had tossed in a trash can out of despair. In this moment, Gaddis affirms the power of Art to stand alone, even to atone for a world gasping from JR's "holy shit."

The aptness of Gaddis's taking on the *Ring* myth reveals itself in other ways, too. Wagner was exiled from Germany during the 1850's for his socialist activities, and this opposition to the ills of capitalism, which first took shape in a pamphlet attacking the corruption of Art by monetary values (*Art and Revolution*, written in 1849), soon took dramatic form in the *Ring* cycle. His librettos center on renunciations of love, both fraternal and romantic, in the presence of greed, and this becomes Gaddis's main theme in *JR*, where love is all just money and calculated talk. We see it in numerous adult characters such as Amy Joubert, Jack Gibbs and Tom Eigen, all of whom haggle over their divorce settlements. Usury also subverts the children's love. When Marion Eigen asks her son David, "Do you love me?" he replies that he does, yet the child acts bewildered when she asks further, "How much?": "Some money . . . ?", he wonders (p. 267). Gaddis is careful, like Wagner, to put the blame for this depreciation on the parents. Bast, for example, inherits the struggle in his artistic soul from his father and grandfather, and from a division in his entire family between beauty and business, just as Siegfried inherited his struggle and loss from Siegmund and Wotan.

Yet Gaddis needs to take another step. Perhaps because there is no symbol within *Der Ring des Nibelungen* for the triumph of Art over Money, Gaddis steps outside Wagner's myth to consider the composer himself. Like Wagner, Bast becomes a true artist because he translates the experience of monetary corruption first into a kind of exile, when he refuses to speak with any of the people around his hospital bed, and the next into works of Art. Bast's finished compositions symbolize the power of Art to transform waste and strife into harmony. They are loving acts.

But there exists a blacker dilemma. *JR* argues that usury and strife are conditions of Nature, even language, which threatens to leave Art very little indeed. In this debate Jack Gibbs plays interlocutor, a role so large and overwhelmingly cynical in the novel that he almost dominates the book, like Satan in *Paradise Lost*. As the disintegrating moral center in this book, Jack's mind, like his coat pockets that bulge from a salmagundi of random notesheets, bursts with disparate knowledge only Gaddis can form into art. Jack's frenzied expostulations on Empedocles and entropy deepen our sense of Wagner's twilight age and argue that the cosmos as a whole is running down from sheer use.

Empedocles first enters *JR* by way of a bogus Greek inscription over the school entrance way—"ΕΒΦΜ ΣΑΟΗ ΑθθΦΒΡ" (p. 20)—which is not only meaningless, it is also unpronounceable. Jack supplied it to the blockheads running the school. They don't know what it might be, yet they admire the grandeur of the Greek letters anyway and one even proposes to use it as the epigraph of his "psychometric" volume on learning, if he can only find out what it means. So where does it come from? Jack throws out a red herring: "You might try Empedocles . . . I think it's a fragment from the second generation of his cosmology, maybe even the first . . . when limbs and parts of bodies were wandering around everywhere separately heads without necks, arms without shoulders, unattached eyes looking for foreheads" (p. 45; my ellipses).[6] This bait does come from Empedocles, and while Jack's paraphrase is right enough he is intentionally off-track on several counts. The letters mean nothing; Empedocles does shed an interesting light on the world of *JR*, but Jack doubtless has in mind the "third generation" of the cosmology when things are coming apart at the seams, not the first or second generation. Of course the simple point in his joke is that language has disintegrated at the joints, but there is more behind it.

In the first place, Jack probably intends that pied inscription to serve as a curse on the school. In his beautiful study of Greek religions, *Persephone*, Gunther Zuntz describes the Hellenic practice of burying the dead with metal lamellae carrying inscriptions. The so-called Orphic Gold Leaves bore poetic lines while leaden pieces, known as the *defixonum tabellae*, bore inscriptions corrupted beyond sense, like Jack's letters. Zuntz speculates that these were popular charms, "articles of mass consumption; objects of beadle's trade like the pictures of the Madonna and of Saints sold at Roman Catholic churches. This fact . . . implies that they came to be appreciated as material objects rather than as carriers of any words engraved on them."[7] He theorizes that the curses were associated with the myth of Kore's descent into Dis, and that they were doubtless directed against certain of the deceased's survivors aboveground. This supernatural power of the lead lamellae would explain why Jack always thinks of his Greek letters and Empedocles when he rides the subway: "looks like the God damn dawn of the world in here necks without heads, arms seeking shoulders, only God damned person live here's Empedocles" (p. 406). These moments always occur after Jack has left the school, and they suggest that he means to execrate the school administrators' obsession with money (gold). In fact, during one of these underground journeys Jack makes the connection between Empedocles, the subway and his bogus inscription, then notices a vending machine that flattens pennies into lucky charms bearing The Lord's Prayer. The machine has "OUT OF ORDER scrawled across it" (p. 161). At moments like this, signification in *JR* seems to spread wall-to-wall.

In the second place, Jack's references to Empedocles dovetail neatly with the "Twilight of the Gods" motif from Wagner and, as we will see, with Jack's ideas on entropy. In Empedocles's cyclical cosmology the world-process is governed by opposing forces of Love (Amity), and Hatred (Strife). The process begins, and ends, in a condition he terms the "Sphairos," or sphere, an apex of creation where no elemental distinctions exist, no differentiations of beings, no becoming or decaying. It represents a starting point in the cosmic cycle, because the workings of Strife in the first generation begin to differentiate reality until, in the second, Amity brings balance and harmony, eliminating monsters that grew when disparate limbs attached themselves to the wrong bodies. Thirdly, Strife reasserts its power and once again the cosmos enters a disintegrating, twilight age before, at the last, being again expresses itself as a Sphairos. Now Jack suggests to the dunces running the school that they should try Empedocles's "second generation . . . maybe even the first," but there are some interesting distinctions arising here. With one hand Jack is surely playing to their eternal optimism about education (a business) and how it brings order and harmony to the mind, while with the other hand he is surely pointing to the third generation, of Strife, which Empedocles describes as a "joyless place" where "works without result run away like water," a place of wrath, greed, envy and sickness. It is a place where Ugliness has defeated Beauty, Talk has drowned out Silence, and Greed has killed Love. Empedocles calls these adverse qualities "Banes," and nothing could more accurately describe the grim conditions at the school JR attends.

Not only the school but the world of *JR* fits this description. In the 96th Street apartment where Bast tries unsuccessfully to work, broken faucets gush water. Characters in the novel are poisoned by mindless talk. Ugliness abounds and both Gibbs and Bast fall ill with pneumonia, a disease of the breath, or spirit, that leaves them temporarily, blessedly, and ironically speechless. Gibbs signifies this stage of decay with every drunken tirade against the usurious chaos surrounding him and his group of friends, but the progress of his own life parallels all three of Empedocles's generations. It corresponds to the first when, early in the novel, he sees around him the strivings indicative of "the dawn of the world." Midway through the novel he falls passionately in love with Amy (Amity) Joubert, and for the space of a week he is at ease and quiet. He even renews himself for work on his monumental book on "mechanization and the arts." Next, when Amy departs for Europe to settle her divorce, Jack settles into the chaos of the 96th Street room, water leaking everywhere (entropy), and there he tries to work alongside Bast. Nothing comes of it because Strife has reasserted its power. Jack's self crumbles under distrust both of Amy's motives and his Big Book, as one of the wayfarers in the room notes when she claims that "nothing's holding him together man she's why he hates it!" (p. 613). Having come that far around the cosmic cycle, Jack feels himself an epigone waiting in despair for the inevitable end.

When he is with Bast, Gibbs tries incessantly to explain this sense of futility, his sense that the depreciation around them is connected with a larger cycling against which they are impotent. Jack believes he has leukemia, a perfect metaphor of entropic, usurious, cancerous Nature. Yet he goes further and argues that the cancer extends to language, to the act of writing. Composing a book in these times, he argues, compares to nursing a terminally ill patient:

> . . . like living with a God damned invalid sixteen years every time you come in sitting there waiting just like you left him wave his stick at you, plump up his pillow cut a paragraph add a sentence hold his God damned hand like warm milk add a comma slip out for some air pack of cigarettes come back in right where you left him, eyes follow you around the room wave his God damned stick figure out what the hell he wants, plump the God damned pillow change a bandage read aloud move a clause around wipe his chin new paragraph God damned eyes follow you out stay a week, stay a month whole God damned year think about something else, God damned friends asking how's he coming along expect him out any day don't want bad news no news rather hear lies, big smile out any day now, walk down the street God damned sunshine begin to think maybe you'll meet him cleared things up got out by himself come back open the God damned door right where you left him. . . . (p. 603)

Jack's Big Book will never get up and walk, and this is precisely why Bast's departure from his hospital bed, finished musical scores in hand, is so important. It is his triumph over corrupt Nature.

From Empedocles's twilight age of Strife the next turn of Nature's wheel is inescapable: the world will become a Sphairos, and while Jack's favorite Pre-Socratic hadn't much to say about its qualities, entropy theory provides him a cogent metaphor of this utlimate *Götterdammerung*. As his name implies, Jack closely follows the theories of Josiah Willard Gibbs, whose *On the Equilibrium of Heterogeneous Substances* set forth the proposition that closed systems, such as the universe, tend ineluctably toward a virtual state of unchanging homogeneity, or "heat death." In *JR*, this is Wagner's fiery ending and Empedocles's Sphairos rolled into one. What is more important, the applications of entropy to information theory (by Norbert Wiener, for example) supplies Gaddis a brilliant analogy for the commerce in Nature of which discourse is simply an aspect.[8]

Jack introduces the theory in his classroom:

> All right let's have order here, order. . . . Before we go any further here, has it ever occurred to any of you that all this is simply one grand misunderstanding? Since you're not here to learn anything, but to be taught so you can pass these tests, knowledge has to be organized so that it can be taught, and it has to be reduced to information so that it can be organized do you follow that? In other words this leads you to assume that organization is an inherent property of the knowledge itself, and that disorder and chaos are simply irrelevant forces that threaten it from outside. In fact it's exactly the opposite. Order is a thin, perilous condition we try to impose on the basic reality of chaos. (p. 20; my ellipses)

This description fits countless situations in *JR*: not only schools but also big business, marriages, families, language, even the isolation artists seek for their work. It would be needless to detail the full extent of Gaddis's analogy to entropy; we need mainly to acknowledge two principal features of the metaphor, which are its imagery of closure and the idea that any intrusions of ordering intelligence result in an increase of entropy.

Begin, as Gaddis does, with the Bast family. From the chaotic table-talk of Edward's great aunts in the opening scene of the novel, it is possible to derive a geneology, which looks like this:

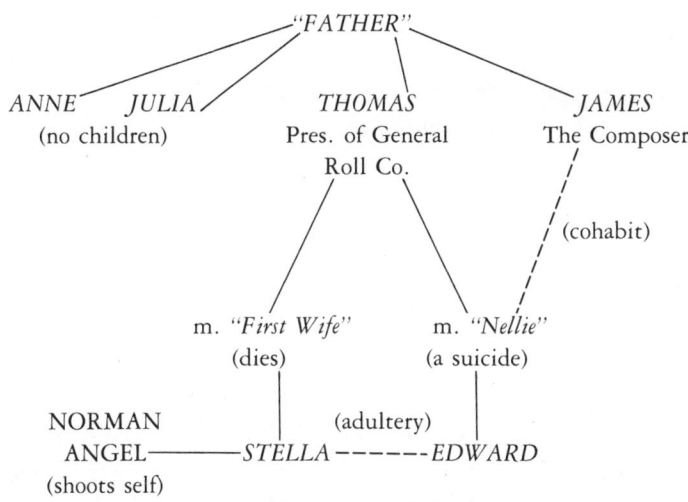

This is a phenomenally closed system held together by near-incestuous liaisons, as well as by a fundamental split between Art and Commerce. Edward's grandfather was both a musician and an entrepreneur; he started the family business of making piano rolls, and he also used to pay his children for improving their musical talents. In his two sons that split widens, because Thomas becomes head of the General Roll Company (mechanized art) while James develops into a famous composer (who, incidentally, happened to be acquainted with Richard Wagner's son, Siegfried). This is Edward's legacy and, as *JR* begins, the circumstance of Thomas dying intestate opens a host of legal and characterological cruxes. Is Edward the son of Thomas, or James's son from his cohabitation with Nellie? Who has controlling interest in the General Roll Company, if Edward has a legal claim to both Thomas's and James's shares? (This is what has Stella worried.) As the name suggests, Edward stands as "beneficiary" of the Bast wealth, but is it an artistic or commercial patent he shall be heir to? This is a beautifully intricate beginning to the novel. Gaddis introduces here the controlling tension between Art and Money; he will soon map Wagner's generations of mythic heroes onto the Bast family tree; and he develops within this family an hilarious example of the closed entropic system. For when the lawyer, Cohen, intrudes to begin sorting things out—"The law seeks order, Miss Bast. Order!" (p. 8)—the only result of his labors is the promulgation of misinformation and strife, as when Stella seduces Edward with the odious intention of wheedling some stock certificates out of him.

The rule is basic to entropy and information theories in general: any attempt to decrease the entropy of a system must involve an operation of ordering (acquiring information), which in turn adds energy to the system, leading to an increase of entropy. This is why Maxwell's Demon never completes his task. In trying to sort Maxwell's hypothetical molecules, the Demon has to expend energy in the form of work, and thus he creates an equal or even greater degree of chaos by the very act of trying to set Nature in order.

And what is J. R. Vansant, if not a type of the sorting demon? His dream is to be "inside" the nerve-center of Commerce, yet at work JR is simply a classic instance of the middleman who arranges transactions and takes his usurious cut. The result is a disorder "whose dramatic repercussions could be felt throughout the corporate world." But it is all an illusion, as Gibbs says, that we superimpose on "the basic reality of chaos," a point Bast tries in vain to make JR acknowledge: "there isn't any inside!" he says, "the only inside's the one inside your head" (p. 644).

The same rule obtains in close systems throughout *JR*. At the school: Hyde dithers reduntantly on about how "in-school tv, to be in-school tv, it has to be in-school with lessons piped into school receivers in school classrooms" (p. 26). Between husbands and wives: Gibbs complains that after a "few years of marriage such a God damned complex of messages going both ways can't get a God damned thing across, God damned much entropy going on" (p. 403). In the 96th Street apartment: Gibbs observes the impossibility of Bast creating anything amidst the noise of a "Radio leaking under there hot water pouring out so God damned much entropy going on think you can hold all those notes together know what it sounds like?" (p. 287). This is why, in *JR*, when artists try to work in isolation they are doomed to failure. They retire to places like Edward's tower, where there exists a "balance between destruction and realization" (p. 69), a place that contains both cast-off music rolls and scrapped opera scores, the detritus of Commerce and Art, and yet this equilibrium collapses the moment Stella Angel steps inside with a purpose in mind. All of Jack's artist friends try to isolate themselves, ending in failure, despair, or suicide. Like Hart Crane, whose businessman father implored his son to come back to Cleveland and leave off writing useless poems, Jack's friend Schramm tries to slam the door on a millionaire father rather than haggle with him about making artworks, but he winds up leaping out a window to his death. This group is not simply lost, as Jack realizes, they are in his words an entire "Turschluss generation."

"Money . . . ? in a voice that rustled": with this first phrase in *JR*, Gaddis indicates that he means to question our assumptions about money and language. And with JR's repeated needling of Bast—"I just thought maybe we could use each other you know?"—the context of that original query widens until it includes all of Art in its relations to Commerce. One answer we can now consider is that the two are virtually equivalent, that money as a semiological system compares with the semiological systems of writing, painting, music, even for that matter the physiochemical system underpinning all Nature. Faced with that realization, the artist becomes an anachronism if he does not acknowledge the universality of usury in all he knows and makes. His precious romanticist notions about how "All art depends upon exquisite and delicate sensibility and such constant turmoil must ultimately be destructive" (p. 289); his desire to be original, as the Romantics understood that term; and lastly his expectation that in Nature he shall learn harmony: all of that melts away. The dilemma remaining is a quintessentially Postmodern formulation. For here is a novel in which people are feverishly imploring each other, over a ceaseless din, to "Listen!", and yet their only recourse *appears* to be, as George Steiner has observed in another connection, a profound silence.

Gaddis's answer is that one should slam neither one's door nor one's mouth. While Bast lies sick in his hospital bed, he listens speechlessly to a fellow patient with the wonderful name of Isidore Duncan, a man whose career—and Bast knows it—was demolished by the JR Family of Companies. Duncan reviles the world for the full range of sins we have witnessed in the novel, and he does so in the most coherent, uninterrupted discourse of the book. His theme, like Gibbs's, is the utter depreciation of value. Bast listens to these tirades with one ear and with the other attends to the music in his mind, a kind of split he has been well conditioned to, and the result is a sheaf of musical compositions that Duncan appreciates and encourages. Bast doesn't speak for some time, and then it is to agree with Duncan that nothing may be worth undertaking because the world only uses things up anyway. It takes several paragraphs of this before Bast realizes that Duncan has died in the night and he has been speaking to a corpse. Bast tosses his musical scores away, then feels a change of heart. I think what happens at this moment is that something Gibbs once told him has finally taken hold. Months previous, Gibbs had advised Bast that "the better among us bear each other in mind" (p. 290). And it rings true. For all his cynicism and fruitless effort, the one redeeming quality in Jack Gibbs is his compassion. For compassion is the imaginative exchange Usury cannot touch, and no doubt that is what Duncan had in mind when he advised Bast that "if you want to make a million you don't have to understand money, what you have to understand is people's fears about money" (p. 683). What people fear is the renunciation of love symbolized in the gnomish creature of J. R. Vansant.

At the last, Edward Bast's compositions can stand on their own for the delightfully human reason that a ruined manufacturer from a place called Zanesville liked the idea of his making them. The artist need not put his work in bondage to any interest beyond that, or to any interest beyond the work's recognition of its own design. Such recognitions, as Gaddis made abundantly clear in his first novel, come from the artist's assimilation of the past, even, one must say, his use of it, and it is only in this sense that the artist breaches Oscar Wilde's dictum: "All art is quite useless."

Gaddis's work is faithful to these precepts in every detail. *JR* is long, and it is difficult as Big Books tend to be. It tries our patience with every turn and transition. Yet if we can appreciate the art of Wagner's *Der Ring des Nibelungen* I believe we may come to appreciate *JR* in a similar spirit. *JR* is an astonishing book, and given the attention equal to the patient decades over which it was composed, this novel yields.

NOTES

1. The published criticism on Gaddis: Joseph S. Salemi, "To Soar in Atonement: Art as Expiation in Gaddis's *The Recognitions*," *Novel*, 10 (1977), 127–36; John Stark, "William Gaddis: Just Recognition," *The Hollins Critic*, 14 (1977), 1–12; Charles Leslie Banning, "William Gaddis's *JR*: The Organization of Chaos and the Chaos of Organization," *Paunch*, 42/43 (1975), 153–65—the only essay, and a very early one indeed, to discuss *JR* at any length.

2. For example, it would be interesting to distinguish the Big Book from what may well be a sub-species—the encyclopedic narrative. Working from Mikhail Bakhtin's seminal study, *Rabelais and his World* (Cambridge, Mass.: M.I.T., 1975), Edward Mendelson begins to define that form during his essay on Pynchon, "Gravity's Encyclopedia," in George Levine and David Leverenz's *Mindful Pleasures: Essays on Thomas Pynchon* (Boston: Little Brown, 1976), pp. 161–95.

3. The transition occurs on p. 18. All references to *JR* are from the edition published by Knopf (New York: 1975) and will be cited parenthetically in the essay.

4. I have used Stewart Robb's translation of *The Ring of the Nibelung* (New York: Dutton, 1960). This line occurs in "The Rhinegold," Scene One, p. 13.

5. *Ibid.*, p. 92. Bast's recollection of Stella swimming also recalls Sieglinda's statement in Act One of "The Valkyrie": "A brook I looked in / gave back my face— / and now again I behold it; / what once the pool did reveal / now is reflected by you."

6. See *Die Fragmente der Vorosokratiker*, ed. and tr. H. Diels, rev. by Walther Kranz (Dublin/Zurich: Wiedemann, 1952). Jack gives a fair rendering of fragments 57 and 60 of MS 31B.

7. See Guncher Zuntz, *Persephone: Three Essays on Religion and Thought in Magna Grecia* (Oxford: Clarendon, 1971), p. 351. My thanks to Guy Davenport for calling my attention to the Orphic leaves.

8. In an essay on Pynchon, Anne Mangel provides a useful summary of entropy theory and illustrates its power as literary metaphor in contemporary writing. See "Maxwell's Demon, Entropy, Information: *The Crying of Lot 49*," *Triquarterly*, 20 (Winter 1971), 194–208. She points out, for example, that Boltzmann's equation for entropy is identical to the formula for the increase of disorder in information systems.

The Soul's Husband: Money in *Humboldt's Gift*

Steven T. Ryan
Austin Peay State University, TN

Saul Bellow's concern for wealth is unusual in contemporary American fiction. In novels as diverse as Flannery O'Connor's *Wise Blood* and Joseph Heller's *Catch 22*, wealth is used only to indicate an American disease (exemplified by Mrs. Flood and Milo Minderbinder). Since the disease is so obvious and is avoided by the primary characters (Hazel Motes and Yossarian), the novelists are able to dismiss crass materialism in order to focus on more profound aspects of the human spirit. Other talented novelists, such as John Hawkes and Thomas Pynchon, virtually ignore questions of material wealth. The reader must accept that their characters are sufficiently solvent and are preoccupied with more significant problems. The concern for wealth is associated with commercial fiction derived from the old schools of realism and naturalism and is thus considered beneath the dignity of serious fiction—including serious, comic fiction.

Bellow's respect for Theodore Dreiser reveals his uncharacteristic regard for naturalism.[1] His concern for money matters can be partly attributed to a modified naturalism in his own fiction. However, Bellow's use of money is far more complex than Dreiser's. Since early in his career, he has used the American dollar as what his character, Humboldt, calls "the soul's husband."[2] In Bellow's view, modern man cannot free himself from the money world by pursuing the ideals of creativity, freedom, goodness, and love. Spirit and matter are wed, and money is the modern essence of matter. For Bellow, the human spirit is "out there," wed with matter. It reveals itself in the most materialistic pursuits of modern man.

In a 1951 short story entitled "Looking for Mr. Green," Bellow presents a modern version of the heroic quest.[3] A young intellectual, Raynor, is employed by the government to deliver checks in the slums of Chicago. The Blacks do not trust him; therefore, he receives no assistance. After repeated failures, he becomes obsessed with the delivery of a single check to a Mr. Green. The delivery of the check becomes a search for the truth. As Raynor views the urban ruins, he attempts to penetrate appearances and discover reality. He sees the urban world as a world constructed on a "convenant." Thus the society agrees to create millionaires. But Raynor cannot decide if the poverty surrounding him is also a product of this covenant. The appearance of the urban world becomes inseparable from the reality of man in nature. In the end, Raynor must compromise by giving the check to an enormous, drunken, nude woman. He can only hope that she will give it to Mr. Green—if Mr. Green actually exists. Both the check and the name, Mr. Green (suggesting greenbacks and verdant nature), demonstrate Bellow's early use of money images in association with a serious, spiritual quest. The truth pursued is two-sided: it is the spiritual truth of the highest ideals and the physical truth of natural forces. But in Bellow's anthropological view, man's civilization, although based on some form of convenant, is yet an integral part of natural forces. The millionaire and his green bills become more accurate metaphors for present natural forces—closer to the essence of nature—than the naturalistic wolf and his red fangs.

In another early story, "The Gonzaga Manuscripts" (1954), a young intellectual, Clarence, quests for the manuscript of a poet whose poems express the reality beneath all appearances. In Madrid, Clarence discovers that Gonzaga's life was as sordid as any man's, and, furthermore, his pure poems were buried with his lover. Clarence is mistaken for a rich American and realizes that he has been bidding for pitchblende mining stock instead of the love poems.

Ideas from both of these early stories carry over into Bellow's later works. The pursuit of money associated with the pursuit of spiritual ideals occurs in *Seize the Day* through the relationship of Tommy Wilhelm and the philosophical con-artist, Dr. Tamkin, and again in *Mr. Sammler's Planet* with the death of Elya and the search for his buried treasure. However, it is in *Humboldt's Gift* that Bellow consistently associates money as a motivating factor with a search for man's immortal spirit. Like "Looking for Mr. Green," *Humboldt's Gift* presents the covenant as an economic agreement associated with a more profound truth. The primary action of the novel is a product of the blank-check covenant between Humboldt and Citrine. The covenant is intended to establish a spiritual bond of "blood brothers." Also, as in "The Gonzaga Manuscript," a young intellectual sees in a poet the expression of the human spirit and pursues the poet to discover his secret. However, again the pursuer discovers a sordid life and financial schemes which cannot be disentangled from the dead poet and his dreams.

The extent to which money controls the action in *Humboldt's Gift* may not be immediately recognized, since Charles Citrine, as narrator, continually shifts the reader's attention to his theorizing, in particular, his "anthroposophic" theory of man's immortal spirit. However, even aside from the blank-check covenant of the past, Citrine's present is a progression of adventures, each of which involves money problems. The present action of the novel can be divided into the following adventures: (1) In Chicago, the petty gangster, Cantabile, beats Citrine's Mercedes-Benz with baseball bats because Citrine stopped his check of $450 for poker winnings. When Citrine gives Cantabile the money, Cantabile takes Citrine from the Russian Baths to the Playboy Club to the top of a new highrise, where he makes paper gliders of the fifty-dollar bills. (2) Citrine, after briefly returning to his apartment, proceeds to the divorce court where he discovers that this ex-wife, Denise, demands more money, and Urbanovich, the judge, intends to place a bond on his money to keep him from skipping the country. (3) Citrine meets with Thaxter who confirms that their publication, *The Ark*, will not appear in spite of Citrine's investments. Thaxter also presents new money schemes, including a tour guide of Europe. (4) Cantabile kidnaps Thaxter and Citrine to use them in his threat on Stronson, a crooked investor who has conned him. Citrine is arrested as a hit man. (5) Citrine is rescued by Stronson's secretary, the daughter of his first love, Naomi. He visits Naomi, a past beauty he lost because of his poverty and his abstract mind (just as he will soon lose Renata). (6) Citrine goes to New York with Renata and has four confrontations: Renata argues for marriage, but Citrine fears that she only wants his money; Humboldt's uncle turns over papers left to Citrine but wants a cut of any profits; Thaxter claims that he has made an agreement with a publisher who will pay Citrine's expenses in Europe; and Kathleen, Humboldt's widow, tells Citrine that she has been given the same film plot as a legacy. (7) Citrine goes to Texas where his brother, Julius, will have open-heart surgery. His brother manages a large property purchase, offers Citrine a cut, and also offers Citrine his wife and fortune if he dies. (8) Citrine goes to Madrid and stays at the Ritz, where the last of his money is squandered since Thaxter has actually made no deal with a publisher. Renata never arrives since she has married the rich Flonzaley. (9) Citrine moves to a *pensión*, and

Cantabile arrives to inform him that a movie has been made from the plot formulated by himself and Humboldt. They fly to Paris to meet with lawyers, and Citrine's security is assured as he also arranges the sale of the film plot left to himself and Kathleen. (10) In the spring, Citrine fulfills his promise to Humboldt's uncle by having Humboldt properly reburied and by turning over half of his profits to the uncle.

This outline is skeletal and does not include Citrine's repeated shifts to the past nor his lengthy discussions of boredom, sleep, and the soul; however, it does present the important movements of Citrine from one place and one meeting to another. Money is important in each adventure. The first three adventures all mark the steady decline in Citrine's fortune as Cantabile, Denise, and Thaxter help reduce the wealth which resulted from Citrine's Broadway hit, *Von Trench*. The four meetings in the New York adventure (6) are used to prepare the reader for the downfall and moderate recovery of Citrine's fortune. In the climax of the novel (9), the downfall is quickly followed by the recovery. Clearly, Citrine's life can never free itself from the influence of wealth.

However, the novel does not present a deterministic view of life. Each of the ten adventures combines money matters with a spiritual search. In the first adventure, Cantabile's sailing of fifty-dollar bills reveals that money is merely a vehicle for his human dignity. In the second adventure, Denise continues an odd love-hate relationship with Citrine. She suggests that they reunite, but the lawyer argues that her desire to strip Citrine of his wealth is a form of castration. In the third adventure, Citrine still honors his friendship with Thaxter while also realizing that Thaxter is financially using him. Their publication, *The Ark*, is supposedly an outlet for such unsellable ideas as Citrine's study of boredom. But this idealistic publication is another scheme depleting Citrine's funds. Bellow achieves his comic effect by this incongruent pairing of the dollar with man's highest ideals. Citrine is pulled apart by greed, gold-digging, gratification on the one side and loyalty, intellect, love on the other. Each of the four meetings in the New York adventure demonstrates this tension. Renata, Humboldt's uncle, Thaxter, and Kathleen speak equally to Citrine's heart and wallet; he can never separate matters of economic survival from matters of human love. Characters like Cantabile, Renata, and Julius are driven by an actual lust for money, yet Citrine does not dismiss them as shallow materialists; rather, he recognizes that their human attributes are hidden beneath their materialism. Cantabile and Julius both maintain hard exteriors and actually are motivated by ruthless greed. However, Citrine sees that they are capable of grand human gestures and acts of love. Renata is a gold-digger, yet her concern for Citrine seems authentic. These characters are not sentimental portrayals of tough hides and soft hearts, nor are they vicious, Hogarthian caricatures. Rather, they live within personal contradictions of hardness and softness with no awareness of the contradictions. In these characters, there exists an unconscious marriage of love and greed.

Citrine is different only because the soul and money create a conscious struggle, whereas with the unconscious characters, the soul and the money are innocently accepted as harmonious. When Cantabile, Julius, and Renata discuss wealth, they are also discussing matters of the soul. Cantabile takes Citrine into his money schemes, and Charles is "perfectly aware that in business Chicago it was a true sign of love when people wanted to take you into money-making schemes" (p. 170). Similarly, Julius can only express his brotherly love by letting Charles in on his construction schemes. Renata experiences a nearly divine bliss when she hears money discussed: "Renata's face, when I recited figures and percentages, was wonderfully at peace" (p. 340). Renata assumes that she can return love for financial security. For her there is no contradiction, but for Citrine the entanglement of money and the human soul is nearly unbearable. Yet Citrine recognizes the same entanglement within himself.

For example, Cantabile, Julius, and Renata all see an automobile as a symbol of their success. It becomes an extension of themselves and as such possesses a spiritual aura. Cantabile has and *is* his white Thunderbird, just as Julius has and *is* his black Cadillac. Renata is ashamed of her aging Pontiac (a remnant of her previous marriage and a suggestion of beauty fading), so she forces Citrine to buy a silver Mercedes-Benz. But when Cantabile abuses this car, it is Citrine who is personally as well as financially offended: "The elite machine, no longer new but worth eighteen thousand dollars three years ago, had been mauled with a ferocity difficult to grasp—to grasp, I mean, even in an esthetic sense, for these Mercedes coupes are beautiful, the silver-gray ones in particular" (p. 33). Citrine reacts just as the other characters would, but then he analyzes his reaction: "I had allowed the car to become an extension of my own self (on the folly and vanity side), so that an attack on it was an attack on myself" (p. 35). This awareness separates Citrine from the other characters, but it does not purify him. He is still left with this odd marriage, both within his environment and within himself. The marriage of the human soul and money is the basis of his obsession with success and failure. He cannot convince himself that his true worth as a human spirit is not somehow related to his financial holdings. His dwindling fortune produces the fear that his spirit is also declining.

One must carefully assess Citrine's attitude towards wealth. He can be categorized as a reliable narrator, but his reliability is limited by his desire to convince himself and his audience that money is not important. Against Humboldt's accusation that he has no right to be so rich, Citrine quickly defends himself by insisting, "money wasn't what I had in mind. Oh God, no, what I wanted was to do good" (p. 2). However, he can seldom keep his mind off money; the worries are as persistent as his dreams of an immortal spirit. Although he cannot hang onto money, he also cannot stop calculating his losses. He knows exactly how much he lost in each venture, and he repeatedly states the amount of money Humboldt took from him down to the exact penny. When he will not admit his money woes, characters like Renata and Kathleen remind him that his worries are revealed in his scrutiny of a menu (p. 337) and a bill (p. 363). Citrine does admit that he thinks "too much about money. It's no good trying to conceal it. It's there and it's base" (p. 71). When Humboldt advises Citrine in his final letter not to "get frenzied about money" and to "overcome your greed" (p. 336), we should realize that he has hit upon an authentic weakness. Citrine may know that financial success and failure are not the same as spiritual success and failure, but he still fears that they are somehow related.

Citrine's obsession with Humboldt is partly based upon his fear that material and spiritual failure are related. As a poet Humboldt's early success was both artistic (thus a conquest of the human spirit) and financial (including a position at Princeton). However, Humboldt fails to repeat his early poetic success and becomes a financial failure. As an American artist, he is in the tradition of F. Scott Fitzgerald—an artist preoccupied by the American success dream, yet driven to self-destruction. He is even captivated by the automobile as he becomes "the first poet in America with power brakes" and is "full of the car mystique" (p. 19). The smashing of his Buick Roadmaster coincides with the decay of his creative ability. Later, using the "blood-brother check," he buys a big Oldsmobile. Before his death, he is aware of his absurdity:

> What I thought I was going to do with this big powerful car on Greenwich Street, I can't tell you. It cost me lots of dough to keep it in a garage, more

than the rent in my fifth-floor walk-up. And what happened to this automobile? I had to be hospitalized and when I got out, after a course of shock treatments, I couldn't remember where I left it. . . . But for a while I drove a hell of a car. (p. 329)

Humboldt realizes that the car is the American symbol of success; it is our clearest representation of money as power. His preoccupation with this power is instrumental in his destruction. It is not poverty that seems to destroy Humboldt: it is rather his acceptance that this poverty *means* failure. For Humboldt, his highest ideals of love, art, and freedom are all dependent upon wealth. Thus, for Citrine to prove his love and become Humboldt's blood-brother, he must perform the monetary ritual of exchanging blank checks. Humboldt explains the sacredness of the act when he calls this exchange a "covenant" (p. 125). He explains the connection with freedom in the following terms: "If I'm obsessed by money, as a poet shouldn't be, there's a reason for it. . . . The reason is that we're Americans after all. What kind of American would I be if I were innocent about money. . . . I go along with Horace Walpole. Walpole said it was natural for free men to think about money. Why? Because money *is* freedom, that's why" (p. 153). To Humboldt, the freedom of wealth will in turn mean an abundance of creativity: "With a million bucks, I'll be free to think of nothing but poetry" (p. 153). Ironically, Humboldt is much like such characters as Renata, Julius, and Cantabile. Wealth is expected to take care of the highest ideals; the soul will spread its wings just as soon as Humboldt can win a million-dollar law suit. The only difference is that the American artist-intellectual will attempt to clarify and justify the connection between the dollar and the soul, whereas the other Americans accept without any doubt that the soul will be freed through success.

Humboldt must explain the mystification of money to clarify its connection with the soul. He insists that "in the unconscious, in the irrational core of things money was a vital substance like the blood or fluids that bathed the brain tissues" (p. 233). This mystification might be dismissed as madness, but, if so, it is the madness of the entire modern world. Citrine describes the importance of money in precisely the same terms: "Earlier when I described how George saved Sharon's life when her throat was cut, I spoke of blood as a vital substance. Well, money is a vital substance, too" (p. 71).[4] The elevation of money to vital substance results from the covenant. Humboldt's insistence on the exchange of blank checks is an enactment of a much larger covenant within the society. This larger covenant amounts to an agreement that money *is* a vital substance; that through such a mutual acceptance an urban environment can be constructed, destroyed, and reconstructed; and that some men will rule in this environment while others will be ruled. In Bellow's view, once the covenant has been made, it cannot be dismissed as a mere imposition upon nature. The equation of blood and money is true as long as it is generally accepted. Characters like Renata, Julius, and Cantabile need not think about the covenant since they live unconsciously within a society which has already accepted that money is no less essential—no further from the secret of life—than blood. Humboldt's idea that money and soul are wed has the same accuracy in the modern world as the traditional relationship of body and soul. In his dying hours, Humboldt writes, "Oh! the might of money and the entanglement of art with it—the dollar as the soul's husband: a marriage nobody has had the curiosity to study" (p. 329). Given the concern of this novel, Bellow clearly sees himself as a writer with such a curiosity.

The difficult task for Citrine is not the realization that money now has the importance of vital substance. The difficult task for Citrine is to free himself not through money but from money. Separating himself from his own money is easy, but separating himself from money's power becomes impossible. His obsession with Humboldt's life and death is based on an increasing realization of this power. The ups and downs of Humboldt and Citrine correlate in the following manner:

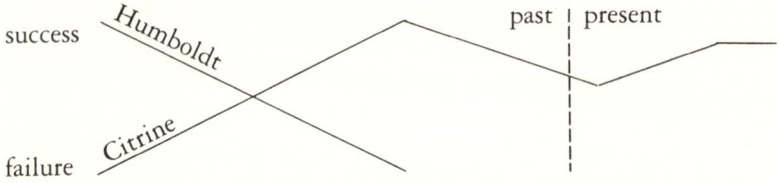

Humboldt's life is the traditional romantic story of an artist reaching success early, declining quickly, and dying young. The first half of Citrine's career is the antithesis of Humboldt's. Citrine begins in the poverty of the Depression and rises to fame and fortune during the fifties. Then, as his fortunes decline, he looks to Humboldt's life and death for help. Like Humboldt, Citrine has become "too paralyzed to write" as he watches his friends and enemies collaborate in emptying his pockets. He realizes that Humboldt destroyed himself by trying to make a killing and begins to realize that everyone's acceptance of money as vital substance is related to Humboldt's destruction. Humboldt was an actor performing a traditional American role. As a modern morality play, his drama proves that money, the soul's husband, is the only true power. Without money, the defenseless soul will be destroyed. Thus, Citrine watches his money disappear and senses his own inclination to live out this drama.

Citrine's investigation of the spirit's immortality becomes his way of struggling against the covenant. He seems to follow the advice he discovered in the writings of Baudelaire: "Whenever you receive a letter from a creditor write fifty lines upon some extra terrestrial subject and you will be saved" (p. 445). When troubled by money, Citrine meditates on the immortality of the soul for at least fifty lines. Standing on his head, he seeks purification. However, the decline continues, and he remains paralyzed. Baudelaire's advice assumes that money and the soul can be divorced by a simple act of the will. Citrine discovers that attempting such a divorce only leads him further into a decline which may actually be spiritual as well as financial.

What Citrine achieves in the end is partly an acceptance of the marriage. By admitting the power of money, Citrine permits the soul to become an active force in the marriage. Significantly, Citrine must leave America in order to strengthen the soul. He first sees his trip to Europe as continued dissipation: "An idiotic old lecher was leaving two children to follow an obvious gold-digger to corrupt Europe" (p. 283). But after squandering his fortune at the Ritz and losing his gold-digger, he relaxes in the lowly *pensión*: "Going broke in a foreign country I felt little or no anxiety. The problem of money was almost nonexistent" (p. 427). In the foreign country, Citrine experiences a weakening of the covenant. He is less inclined to associate his poverty with a failure of the spirit. However, Citrine's transcendental passivity in the *pensión* reveals more suffering than redemption. He is unable to recover from Renata's desertion. His recovery requires the gift of Humboldt, a gift which again merges a monetary and spiritual blessing. The monetary blessing is the profitable movie plots left to Citrine. These plots can make Citrine's fortune, if he is willing to go through a lengthy litigation against the Hollywood plagiarists. The spiritual blessing results from the discovery that Humboldt, in spite of shock treatments, retained the human characteristics which attracted Citrine to him in the beginning. In spite of his money obsession and his mad jealousy, Humboldt had retained his creative gift, as well as his affection for his blood-brother and his wife. Therefore, Citrine need not be haunted by the ragged image of Humboldt the failure. Since Humboldt's soul had not been destroyed by his loss of status, Citrine need not accept his own decline.

At the same time, the combining of the monetary and spiritual blessings forces Citrine to again deal with money as the soul's husband. Humboldt had "kept dreaming about miraculous money until the end. He was dying and still he wanted to make us both rich" (p. 360). The gesture of love is real, but, as in the case of Julius, it finds its expression through money, the vital substance of the modern world. The same combination of soul and money occurs in Citrine's final assessment of Humboldt: "who loved the Good and the Beautiful, and one of whose slighter inventions was entertaining the public on Third Avenue and the Champs-Elysees and earning, at this moment, piles of dollars for everyone" (p. 469). His ideals of "the Good and the Beautiful" are remembered along with his final success. Citrine knows that this "slighter invention" has a real effect on the world around him—the public partakes of Humboldt's invention; it cannot be dismissed as insignificant, nor can this reality be separated from Humboldt's love of goodness and beauty.

The movie plots force Citrine back into this modern reality, as Cantabile, the epitome of the new world, pulls Citrine out of his guru meditations, back into the world of lawyers and lawsuits. Once Citrine returns to this world, he realizes that he must accept the presence of the covenant and its effect on his own character: "I hadn't lost tons of money for nothing. I had mastered the commercial lingo at least. And as Julius had observed, I was a Citrine by birth" (p. 453). He can say that his "own romance with wealth is over" (p. 462), but he grudgingly admits that he cannot divorce himself from his world's idea of reality:

> Business, with the peculiar autonomy of business, went its own way. Like it or not, we thought its thoughts, spoke its language. What did it matter to business that I suffered a defeat in love, . . . that I investigated the doctrines of anthroposophy? Business, sure of its own transcendent powers, got us all to interpret life through its practices. Even now, when Kathleen and I had so many private matters to consider, matters of the greatest human importance, we were discussing contracts options producers and sums of money.(p. 459)

Convinced of its "transcendent power," business continues to treat money as vital substance. Citrine no longer believes that he can or should separate himself from this reality. He knows the danger of the marriage—the danger that the soul's husband will claim all of the power, all of the reality, and will even convince the soul that it is no longer real. However, Citrine argues that observation reveals something beyond verification: "the existence of a soul is beyond proof under the ruling premises, but people go on behaving as if they had souls, nevertheless" (p. 463). Citrine accepts this as the paradox of his world. Humboldt, Renata, Julius, and Cantabile chase money as though this verifiable reality were the only reality, yet, even while in the midst of their pursuits, they all reveal the existence of a soul.

Citrine's own solution is to make peace with the business world. He will not pursue the million-dollar lawsuit of Humboldt's dreams, nor will he remain on his head in the *pensión* and ignore the plagiarism. He decides to make a deal which will modestly provide for himself, Kathleen, Humboldt's uncle, Humboldt's body, and even Cantabile. He will invest his share with his brother and live off the interest. He will also accept a bit role in a movie (the acceptance of a social performance without demanding a lead role), and he will continue his study of the immortal spirit. By such a compromise, he will not break the covenant. He accepts that money has become a vital substance, an authentic shaper of worldly events. But he permits it only the position of husband, the apparent power and provider. The soul is also real, and its endurance—maybe immortality—easily offsets the dollar's bravado.

NOTES

1. In an interview with Gordon Lloyd Harper, Saul Bellow explains his debt to Dreiser and offers the following praise of Dreiser's work: "he was rich in a kind of feeling which has been ruled off the grounds by many contemporary writers—the kind of feeling that every human being intuitively recognizes as primary. Dreiser has more open access to primary feelings than any American writer of the twentieth century." "Saul Bellow" is an interview from *Writers at Work*: the Paris Review Interviews, Third Series, and is reprinted in *Saul Bellow: A Collection of Critical Essays*, ed. Earl Rovit (Englewood Cliffs, N.J.: Prentice-Hall, Inc., 1975), p. 7.

2. Saul Bellow, *Humboldt's Gift* (New York: Avon Books, 1976), p. 329. All future references to *Humboldt's Gift* will be from this edition with page numbers included parenthetically in the text.

3. Eusebio L. Rodrigues offers a fine analysis of this story's use of the quest in an article entitled "Koheleth in Chicago: The Quest for the Real in 'Looking for Mr. Green,' " *Studies in Short Fiction*, 11 (Fall, 1974), 387–93.

4. A similar elevation of money to the level of a basic human mystery is apparent in the following quotation from *The Adventures of Augie March*: "Here was vast humankind that meshed or dug, or carried, picked up, held, that served, returning every day to its occupations, and being honest or kidding or weeping or hypocritic or mesmeric, and money, if not the secret, was anyhow beside the secret, as the secret's relative, or associate or representative before the peoples" (New York: Fawcett World Library, 1953), p. 359.

Things I Left Out of My Autobiography
or
How Thorstein Veblen's Theory of Conspicuous Consumption Worked for Me

Mark Harris
Pittsburgh, PA

"Money is all, practically and in the Marxian sense."
—Edgar Lee Masters, in *Vachel Lindsay*

They seemed so awfully to want him. The candidate arrived on a cold day and they did everything to keep him warm, quartering him in Room 1004 (he was a Diary keeper, recording for the ages important facts like room numbers) of the Webster Hall Hotel, soon thereafter run out of business. Its trade was mainly academic travelers, students, and old folks at home—Stephen Foster lived most of his life in The Smokey City—classes of people ambitious hotels despise: hotels want drinkers on expense accounts.

When the hotel was run out of business the candidate, who was a writer, and who by then had lived for two years in that city, wrote an essay about its passing in the magazine named for the city itself, whose editor had *also* seemed so awfully to want him. The editor had hired him over lunch with a handshake, and afterward fired him in the same restaurant, saying "You're a luxury I can't afford." What did the editor mean by that? Was the candidate too expensive, too oblique, too academic, too subtle?

To the candidate himself his own prose seemed enormously comprehensible—a fucking *baby* could understand every word he wrote. But the editor was no baby. The editor had been paying the candidate $150 a month for a thousand words, upon which the candidate worked (apart from reflection and research) two days a months. It was one of a number of sums floating to the candidate apart from his salary, it gave to his life a liberating working margin, and by reason of his super-solvency he was a happy person. More than one of his intellectual friends had said to him, "You're the only happy person I know."

The magazine was trendy, snappy, slangy, yearning to be timely. No doubt the candidate was too inward for it. He had often fallen out of favor on that account. Years earlier, by unconscious natural selection, he had fallen into university life and remained there, where incomprehensibility was understood to be no necessary liability—that's what scholars were for, to clear up the incomprehensibility as time went by, to make today's mystery tomorrow's commonplace.

How they cheered me that day at the Webster Hall Hotel! . . . I came as a candidate for a job, Flight 90, TWA, Sunday afternoon, January 12, 1975 . . . carried . . . through a snowstorm from the airport, and as we entered the lobby of the hotel the voices of guests and employees alike roared out in jubilation. People jumped up and down, blew horns, rattled noise-makers. In the middle of the lobby floor, upright and abandoned, stood an old lady's "walker," as they are called, the lady herself having sailed away under her own power, rejuvenated by my coming. Coincidentally, during that hour news had also arrived . . . that the Steelers, a football team of which I was barely aware, had defeated its rival at the Super Bowl.

That night the candidate went with Professor Abba to his house, sitting a long time with him and his wife. Later in the evening they were joined by Professor Beeba and *his* wife. The candidate was the soul of amiability, serenity, humility. He kept referring to himself as a school-teacher rather than a writer, he thought people ought to be teachers first and writers by chance, if that was how things worked out for one (as it had for him). One ought not to write for money, he said, the world of commerce was spiritually barren, the world of *academe* he lauded. They liked him. (In an interview with Saul Bellow someone reported someone's saying of another writer, "Oh, I met him once, he seemed nice enough." Bellow replied, "We all do, until you get to know us.")

Back in his warm room in the Webster Hall Hotel the candidate wrote in his Diary, "It was a most engaging evening." Explain then why things begun in such warmth of engagement froze forever in hatred, strife, and fear, filling the air with dirty names. Professor Beeba has since risen at a Department meeting to call the candidate "dishonest." The candidate was pleased when the Department Parliamentarian declared the raging Beeba out of order. Nowadays, the candidate and Professor Beeba scarcely speak to each other. When Professor Beeba sees the candidate his face grows white with an anger to which he is unaccustomed.

Professor Abba, on the other hand, speaks to the candidate when they meet. The two men exchange pleasant thoughts and ideas, but they are socially distant. Professor Abba is a brilliant, somewhat sequestered man who had thought at the beginning that his relationship with the candidate (if the candidate remained) would be much richer than it has been: he had hoped that the candidate would inspire him, set him afire, but that has not occurred, the candidate has been a disappointment to Professor Abba, who perhaps also thinks of him as, in a way, dishonest. He has not said so aloud, however, as Professor Beeba did—only to be ruled out of order by the fair-minded Parliamentarian.

On the second day of the candidate's visit he—this is once again his Diary—"met with faculty informally this morning." Mainly he sat, as he recalled, in a room he never thereafter identified with certainty, where he drank several cups of coffee and carried forward a marathon conversation with faculty members who came and went between their classes. Several of them mentioned having met him here or there about the country, and although the candidate could not in all cases recall the persons he said he did, feeling himself making the motions of sidewalk politics.

When lunchtime came he walked several blocks down the street with faculty members to a restaurant known as The Black Angus. He returned to that restaurant many months later with a professor—a writer—who intended to resign her appointment. The candidate tried to dissuade her, urging her "to swallow her pride." "Do you think I'm Deep Throat?" she inquired by way of reply, and subsequently resigned in spite of the candidate's continued argument to the effect that a writer ought to remain academically connected.

He himself would never quit. Surely he would never leave one academic job before being certain of another. He required that paycheck, without which he could not write; and if he could not write he was unhappy. That was how he had come to live over the years. He thought of himself as a good and growing writer whose growth had been made possible by security; by the leisure which security provided. Looking back upon his life, especially through his fiction, he saw that the center of his writing was the story of the hero seeking safety with honor. As often as not, his heroes romantically renounced money. But the candidate himself had not, and over the years in one way or another he had said to hundreds of students—paraphrasing, he believed, Thoreau—"Do not live by the work of your hands." He saw dozens and dozens of young men and women, all of whom could write rather well, fly away on the wings of optimism, encouraged by some first success, some first astounding paycheck. Now they were the real thing, the "pro." They sped to New

York, Los Angeles, and the candidate knew there was nothing he could say to stop them. Even so, he said it, and frequently repeated it, "Don't be a 'pro.' Get steady money. That is the only way to find out how good you are."

On the second night the candidate wrote in his Diary, "Everything went very well. Cold weather." No problems, everything going very well, everybody loving the candidate to pieces. Here he would find happiness exceeding even the happiness he had brought with him. Here was virtue rewarded. God bless America, it paid a fellow in the long run for his earnest work, his hard-won writings. They loved him in—Or had they read his writings at all? He had had the experience of retroactive anger: of people reading his books afterward and telling him he had deceived them before; of people discovering *post facto* in the books the bad character of the author which had escaped their earlier observation.

The dynamics of the Department were such that the candidate was in demand. Many of its members thought he would do them good, lend the Department some element it lacked, animate its members, set its writers on fire, invigorate them, introduce sophistication into the atmosphere, provide marketplace connections. He could feel, from party to party, dinner to dinner, meeting to meeting, that he was a winner. In boyhood terms, he was sweeping the series. His remaining task was to hold his ground, resist erosion, commit no blunders. He forswore clarifications, preferring simply to ignore potential trouble. He had the votes. In the days ahead, between the time of his departure and the time of the Department vote, he'd lose a few. He guessed the final vote at 75%, but he never troubled himself to look it up in the Department minutes, and so he never knew it, even as he never knew who his champion had been in the first place. Was it Professor Abba? It was not Professor Beeba; and it was none of the Thoreauvian Leftist Unionist Marxist Radicals, who in the end were his most natural friends.

On the third day of the candidate's visit he took lunch with prospective colleagues at Stouffer's restaurant where the magazine editor afterward both hired and fired him, and he rode with Professor Abba on a tour of the very neighborhood where he would logically live. Perhaps he passed the very house he would some day call his own, into which he would move with his wife, one son, their cats, their life's paperwork, pieces of art, pieces of furniture, and a wardrobe whose very few choice garments he wore only for special occasions such as a candidate's visit.

The house was located at a comfortable intersection. Hundreds of people would pass his house every day, thinking of him (he hoped) as they passed, admiring the ostentatious modesty of his house lying gracefully low among the steeply rising gables of its neighbors. Often, passing by, his colleagues would see crews of working men clambering about—now painters, now diggers, now gardeners, now tree surgeons, now roofers, now masons. How terribly expensive they must be! How very much trouble to keep up so costly a house! How green the grass was! One wondered how far it extended behind the concealment of the high hedges. How well-kept, how glowingly lit, the man who lives there has undoubtedly been successful at his work! Once upon a time, around the corner, Gladys Schmitt lived in a house she bought with literary royalties. The candidate would hear of this more than once: if literary judgment were uncertain the house, on the other hand, was undeniable. If talent were difficult to assess, real estate was not. Money was the world's view, shared by deans, chancellors, and trustees, who tend to trust a wealthy professor before a merely industrious professor. One thing was certain: here was a candidate the powers would approve.

The final scheduled event of the candidate's visit was a dinner party followed by a reception at the home of Professor Chair. An event of this evening inspired in the candidate's head a story he told three years later in the magazine *Esquire*, for which he received a fee of $2,500 less his agent's commission. The story reflects the dual process characteristic of much of the candidate's fiction: it had been inspired by his distaste for a person of his acquaintance, but it grew to express a larger, repetitive theme of his life. In "Touching Idamae Low" the candidate is disguised as the personnel director for an industrial corporation, who is invited by a rival corporation for "a little get-acquainted visit." Object: a position at a plant farther south, where the golf is better. The candidate, whose name is Auerman, is informed that at this newer and more southern plant "the employees really make the decisions," but Auerman knows better, and the story turns upon Auerman's discovery of the true decision-maker, and how he reacts to her when he realizes the extent of her power.

In the larger sense the story reveals to Auerman and to his creator Auerman's amusing or disgusting capacity for appearing to be one sort of person at a given moment when he is prevailingly another. The candidate had cast Auerman as candidate. No doubt, then, this business of presenting himself as candidate was one which the candidate had entered into with interest. It appealed to him, a harmless sport, like baseball. Not until he had finished writing the story, however, was he conscious of his having played the game so regularly. His fiction often revealed to him in this way who he was, where he had been, and what he had done there.

In his mind's eye as he wrote his story the candidate must have carried images of the dinner party and reception at the home of Professor Chair. It was Professor Chair, executive officer of the Department, who drove the candidate to the airport on the following day. They were alone. The triumph of the Steelers was three days into history. The candidate sensed that Professor Chair was not himself enthused about his candidacy except insofar as the candidacy might reflect the will of the Department. Professor Chair saw his duty in the fulfillment of Department will, unlike the candidate, who saw his duty as the obligation to fulfill his own vision. The candidate had concluded from his practice of literature that popular judgment was defective: popular judgment was money judgment. Even in literature he saw that this was true, and to some extent he relied upon its working for the best: that is to say, an author's merely best-selling work might turn attention to the author's better work. Financial success may ultimately attract critical attention. Money is bait. Money is decoy. Money is the mother of authority. The candidate during all the first half-century of his life had thought of money as an item separate from virtue, but at last he was prepared to accept the idea of money as exchange.

Whether Professor Chair was acquainted with any of the work of the candidate the candidate did not know, nor was he about to ask. He had no intention of embarrassing the executive officer of the Department. He recalled afterward Professor Chair's having complained of a certain writer out of his past that he had wickedly written of events at a certain university where both he and Professor Chair had been employed. The candidate nodded his head as if to condemn such wickedness, but he asked himself inside his nodding head, "Of what can we writers write except of places we have been?" By *been* he meant experience, which "consists," says James, "of impressions . . . impressions *are* experience."

Away flew the candidate. Win or lose, he could say he'd been to The Smokey City, about which he had read so much as a National League boy.

Twenty-two days later, at the instruction of his Department, Professor Chair offered the position to the candidate at a salary of—but there's a problem. Finite sums distract readers. The salary the candidate was offered was neither $1,000,000 nor $10,000. What good will it do the reader to know? One university is not another, one year is not another, and fringe benefits vary. Put it this way: when to the sum he named Professor Chair added $1,000 per year the addition meant very little to the candidate; the effect was similar when Professor Chair added a sum to cover moving costs. The candidate always lost money moving from place to place. His objective was to get there, not to make money in the process. His need was to find and maintain a situation in which he would be free to write. It was the essence of his policy or strategy, such as it was, to insure his freedom and happiness not by negotiating for money but by seeking ideal conditions for work. He sought security, tenure.

When he accepted the job it was not for the money. He wished to be acknowledged not with money but with respect. He hoped people would admire his profound and extended experience of writing. He hoped that his colleagues would not mistake his money for his intention: his intention as a writer had been to change the world. He had begun in idealism, and to a great extent he continued in the same way. He cared for his themes and for the things he felt he knew, not for money, which was but a verifying bonus.

Winter became summer. In August in his gleaming expensive Mercedes Benz automobile the candidate set out from his house in southern California. "I dread the eastern weather," he wrote in his Diary on the eve of departure. "Somehow it's just unbelievable to be going. I expect, however, soon to be excitingly involved." On the following night, in Room 119 of the King's Inn in Kingman, Arizona, he wrote of the road, "It is boring and lonely." For companionship he carried with him a tape cassette into which he spoke many thoughts, only one of which, as far as he knew, was ever of any use to him—a sentence he soon inserted as the first sentence of a languishing novel still uncompleted four years later: "People think that because I live in a big house I cannot be a revolutionary."

On the afternoon of the next day he swung off the Interstate to visit the little town of Thoreau, New Mexico, thinking he might find there a community dedicated to renunciation, the simplification of desires, and the celebration of craftsmanship. He asked several people why the town was named as it was, but almost nobody knew. "It was named for a French poet," one citizen told him. Only the postmaster knew better: it was named for Henry David Thoreau of Massachusetts by someone who admired him.

The candidate passed on to Albuquerque. There he had once attended the University of New Mexico. Near the campus he sat to dinner in an

Indian (of India) restaurant, expecting at any moment to be joined by old friends striding along with their books beneath their arms exactly as he had last seen them thirty years before when he and they formed the Thoreauvian Whitmanian Radical Socialist Marxist Utopian Unionist coalition of the student legislature.

Onward, eastward. He carried in his car three works in various stages of progress. One was the languishing novel-manuscript now supplied with a new first sentence; another was a screenplay adapted from an episode in the life of James Boswell; the third was a sketchy outline of a projected screenplay adapted from Roger Kahn's book, *The Boys of Summer*. It was the third project he attended to first. Money sped him on. He was paid by Universal Films the sum of—but there's the problem again. How much? Say five figures. Five high or five low? Say five middle—paid a sum in five figures for a screenplay he sent by mail to Universal Films, who never announced its receipt nor in any other way acknowledged the existence of either the manuscript or the author. The author had received his money. Universal City knew no other medium of exchange.

Luckily for the candidate his recurring source of support existed elsewhere. But for *academe* he would have been devoured in the jungles of America. Onward, eastward. In Tulsa he was joined by his son, who had flown from camp in California. Soon they arrived at the outskirts of The Smokey City in their dust-covered expensive Mercedes Benz automobile. Here a fantastic downpour washed their car clean, restoring its gleaming.

The candidate attended the year's first department meeting on a lovely autumn morning in a large room in the one-time Schenley Hotel. The hotel was known to him through a moment in Willa Cather's story, "Paul's Case," which he had read many times. It was the story of a boy who had no way of knowing he was an artist, and who was destroyed by the drabness of cultural landscape. Paul was a boy of The Smokey City, and he thought he knew his trouble: he had no money. Wretched analysis, wretched solution: Paul stole money, spent it in a moment, and died immediately.

The candidate sat through three faculty meetings dreaming of the old days of this hotel, when Forbes Field stood across the street. Into these very rooms in this National League city his old heroes wandered in 1937 or thereabouts, Terry, Ott, Travis Jackson, Hubbell, Joe Moore, others, others (they were Giants in those days!), into these corners now occupied by Professors Abba, Beeba, and Chair. To those first Department meetings the candidate, now a tenured voter, wore collar and tie and sat in the posture of an elder statesman, harboring his counsel, swallowing his pride, even as his heart resisted formulations coming at him from the floor. He had the impression afterward that his posture had lasted a year. His Diary knew better. By December he was embroiled, distressed, writing in his Diary, "Things went poorly at a faculty meeting this morning. I felt defeated." By what issue he was defeated he could not recall. There were several.

He recalled in general, however, that the division between his colleagues and himself usually involved questions of hiring, firing, and verification. Some of his arguments were these:

1. The Department should hire faculty from its own ranks.
2. The Department should read candidates' writings regardless of whether the writings are published.
3. Publishing and printing, especially at the commercial centers, are judgments of money, irrelevant to knowledge or art.
4. Journalism is a business, not an art.
5. Visits by candidates are delusional and worthless: the candidate comes to hide, not to be seen.
6. Writing should be taught by persons who have earned Ph.D. degrees. With few exceptions, "professional" writers are worthless to learning. They are interested mainly in money. If they had earned money outside the academy they would never have asked to be in.

These attitudes puzzled or enraged his colleagues, to whom it seemed that the candidate was arguing against himself. They viewed him as paradoxical, whimsical, self-indulgent, nasty, and finally dishonest (although Professor Beeba, on the last point, was ruled out of order by the Department Parliamentarian), for how could it be that the candidate argued against the very criteria serving as his own verification: he had come from a distance, he had been commercially printed, he had written journalistically.

The candidate was prepared to confess that he argued an ideal he had not wholly lived. On the other hand, having *been* there, he felt himself obligated to report his sensations to students and colleagues. He had arrived where he had arrived without necessarily intending to arrive there, but there was in any case a vast difference between one's having arrived and one's directing others, such as students, along an identical path. He did not renounce what he had become. He did not intend (on this point he was challenged) to give his money to charity, roll his Mercedes off a cliff, or permit the grass to overwhelm the garden of his house. If he could not turn back he could at least tell where he had been.

For three years in The Smokey City the candidate continued to issue his writings to the world. Among these were his story, "Touching Idamae Low," other works for which he was suitably paid, and some work for which he received little or nothing. For several full-length works he received nothing at all: they were quickly rejected in the commercial market. He was extremely grateful for his academic situation, perceiving *academe* as the salvation of writers; for that reason he attempted to preserve its purity.

In spite of his good intentions (so he viewed them) his friendship with Professor Abba never developed—Professor Abba never took fire from the candidate. Professor Beeba remained distant. Professor Chair resigned his executive office to return to teaching. He was replaced by Professor Dooda, who was elected to office by votes other than the candidate's: the candidate voted for the Unionist Utopian *etc.*, who finished second in a field of three. After the election the candidate wrote to Professor Dooda, "I did not vote for you but I will help you all I can."

One day, to the candidate's surprise, Professor Dooda urged him to be "happy." He was taken aback. Did she think he was unhappy? Was that the idea people had—that his odd opinions were a symptom of unhappiness? He thought of himself as happy. Thank God for health and the health of his family. Thank God he wrote every day, which was his happiness. Thank God he had a good agent, a good tax man, good friends, a good plumber, a good garage mechanic, a good typewriter repair man, and a good dentist. Was he not writing well and learning things every day? The conflicts of his life, which Professor Dooda seemed to see as evidence of unhappiness, were the very stuff of which his writing was made. That had always been his happiness, to create fiction, to objectify his life by making a story of it, as innocent people tell their dreams to their friends as a means of conveying their tangled thoughts.

Not long after Professor Dooda's monition the candidate resumed writing a novel he had attempted on several occasions of the past. This time it continued and would not stop. He had brooded upon it for ten years. He now completed it in four months. A year after he completed it he read it freshly, as much as possible as if it were someone else's, to discover where he had been, who he was, and what he had done there. "I must tell you how I work," Flannery O'Connor once wrote to her agent.

"I don't have my novel outlined and I have to write to discover what I am doing. Like the old lady, I don't know so well what I think until I see what I say; then I have to say it over again."

In *It Looked Like For Ever* the candidate is disguised as Henry Wiggen, baseball player. Not for twenty-two years had he comfortably worn the uniform of Henry Wiggen, but the present story invited Henry's diction. It called particularly for a casual, frank, direct relationship to money which Henry, in his world, could assume in ways the candidate, in his, could not. Baseball never demands moral purpose.

Henry Wiggen at thirty-nine was prepared to come to terms with his resignation from baseball, but his difficult daughter Hilary screamed herself breathless in protest. She was his youngest, and she had never seen him play.

> "I have never saw you play baseball," she said, "and now I will never see you at all," and she screamed again for quite some time while her sisters and her mother and the servants returned to their various activities. I sat on the steps with Hilary. I removed my coat and gloves and hat. "My dear girl," said I, "you are disgusting and unreasonable. Every ball player arrives some time at his last pitch, and I have arrived at mine."

Did you notice the servants? Henry intended you to notice them. Lying in bed one night in his splendid house in Perkinsville he counted the women who were guests beneath his roof. "That was 10. Counting servants 13." In New York City his apartment, famous for its shower bath, snuggles close to the Waldorf-Astoria. He owns so many stocks he makes jokes of his losses. He rides about with a telephone in his car, which everyone loves to examine. (Whether his automobile was a fabulously glistening Mercedes Benz the candidate never knew: he created the man; only God can create an automobile.)

Most people in baseball love Henry, but almost nobody will hire him. For Hilary, and soon for himself, he suffers disappointment and the pain of pride, from which he can rescue himself by citing his advantages, those symbols of happiness most of his associates view as ends in themselves.

The one baseball manager who wants Henry to play for him is sweet chinless Jack Sprat, who can believe, as almost nobody else can, that the man who has everything truly cares more for his art than he cares for mere material things. Almost alone, Jack Sprat believes in Henry's *motivation* (a word which is always italicized in the book). Sprat's boss, Suicide

Alexander, "the owner of California" (i.e., the owner of a California baseball franchise), is extremely skeptical of his manager's assessment of Henry's *motivation*. Henry is fond of wine, making him in Suicide Alexander's view an esthete, a contented man empty of the young man's beer-drinking *motivation*. Suicide Alexander speaks of money at a funeral, flashing his bankbook to show Henry how much money *he* has, and concluding that Henry's lack of interest in the bankbook is further evidence of Henry's absence of *motivation*. In the end, Henry and Sprat win Suicide Alexander by persuading him that Henry stole his golf clubs. Capitulating, Alexander is jubilant: "Any 39 year old millionaire that will steal a 1/2 a bag of golf clubs off me at a dead man's funeral is my kind of a man."

In 1971 Henry wore $80 sports shoes. His wife, who conducts a money-making school, is author of a book called *Baseball Wives*, which is presumably also money-making. (People believe books earn money: I heard even the worldly baseball man, Leo Durocher, say on television one night that Jim Bouton, baseball player turned writer, "can afford to have zany ideas with his kind of money," as if Bouton's books were necessarily profitable.) Everything Henry touches turns to money. Royalties flow to him by sheerest accident from a child's game called "Heads Up Baseball." For a two-minute film he receives $50,000. For his baseball broadcasts he receives $10,333.33 per night. His family's extravagance is frequently conspicuous: Hilary flies first-class coast to coast so that she has room to spread her books about. Tired of one afternoon of apartment-hunting in Los Angeles, Henry buys a house in Beverly Hills.

What of the candidate, who created Henry Wiggen? Does he too have everything? The candidate knew in the act of writing the impossibility of the reader's sublime detachment. Almost nobody acquainted with an author can read the author's work apart from an image of the author himself-herself. The candidate may therefore have used his art to project both a private message and a public book. Perhaps in projecting his newest Henry Wiggen to the world he was projecting himself also to his colleagues. Was it the shy candidate's intention to speak of himself by speaking of Henry Wiggen? To some extent the candidate creates not only his characters but himself, expressing to his contemporaries the message his characters express to theirs. If Henry flaunts material advantage as a means of compensating himself for spiritual disappointment, the candidate might be doing the very same.

The candidate exaggerates by implication, offering through Henry

Wiggen a version of himself for his colleagues. He was not a student of money, but he knew this much: that if his colleagues believed him to be rich they would turn sooner and more seriously to his opinions than if they believed him to be merely one of them. And of all the grudges he bore his colleagues this was first.

Creatively Writing the Grippingly Erotic True Story
Herbert Gold
San Francisco, CA

"My job was to be faithful to other women's men," she said, and I thought her brilliant and terrific. This lovely young person had a story to tell. She had lived it with her body, and now her way to justify it was to write it. She aroused my interest. For reasons which she named as curiosity plus money she had committed herself to a career as a white slave in a house in San Francisco. "Not a call girl, not a hooker," she said with winsome pedantry. "I was a white slave."

"I think thereupon might hang a tale," I said.

"You will help me bring it to the public?"

"Tell me, tell me," I said. "But you should write it, and I'll help you *after* you write it—you yourself, telling your own story. In the meantime, coffee?"

"I think I might," she said.

She was sleek, neat, tanned, dark, of that black-Irish darkness and bony nose which suggest Spain; and her body was exercised with loving care by herself and perhaps others; and if I had to find a flaw because otherwise I might be too shy with her, it would be the shudder of cheek when she shook her head, a suggestion of jowls in her post-menopausal years—something I would surely never live to see. This would have to do for defect; it was all I could find.

Oh, and perhaps an extra portion of self-love in the pertness on the edge of the chair, so much boiling energy for what she wanted. Well, even I can't call that a flaw. But if I had been younger, her age, the incipient jowl might have made me fall helplessly, hopelessly, in love with her. She would have seemed possible, accessible. But since she was a mere child of twenty-three, one year out of UCLA, I only fell wistfully.... Well, I coveted her distant loveliness, melting in the future like the lip of snow on the windowsills of my ancient childhood in Cleveland.

She explained that *Waiting for Cordelia*, my novel about call persons in San Francisco, made her realize that I am just the one to guide her literary career. Praise makes me purr; I turned strict to control it. We met at Just Desserts. I thought young people and carrot cake and cappucino would be more . . . counterphobic? is that the word?—than drinks in a darkened romantic bar. The bright, Danish and San Francisco, friendly coffee house was a straightforward environment for literary guidance. I could see better here, too.

"How did it happen?" I asked.

"Oh, a stupid summer marriage. Bored. Curious. And I want to write."

"I can understand that," I said soothingly.

"Also a little money never hurts."

"That too I understand," I said, and at this point I did not cover her small white hand with my big brown one. So much sagacity earned a fatherly pat, but even from this I abstained.

"You're such a good listener. People say you're. . ." she said, her voice trailing off. She didn't want to flatter me too much. But I got the idea.

"What was it, can you tell me, point of view?" I asked briskly.

"Well, some of the johns were nice. They weren't cripples and freaks as you might believe. I actually liked some of them. I like sex, by the way."

"Hmm, yes, very good," I said.

"And the madam was okay, too. A nurse. An R.N. from Phoenix. The place was clean. A detail: we couldn't read during working hours. We just had to wait in the parlor and look sexy. They gave us the clothes—bathing suits before five, kind of frilly gowns after dark—another detail."

"Not very *real*, is it?" Oh dear, when I'm nervous I get stupid.

She forgave me. "Reality isn't their shtick. For real love, you go outside. There's always the real world. This is kinks for normal people, you understand?"

"You have a great grasp of the picturesque detail," I said. "I seem to see an intensely dramatic and perhaps ironic . . . when you write it I'll be glad to help. Let's meet as soon as you do."

"I'd say I'm eighty percent there," she said.

"The experience is interesting in itself. That's half the battle."

"Since I was an alleged hooker," she said.

"What? You admit it, you're writing about it."

"Never convicted or even arrested, mister."

"Adolph Hitler, the suspected dictator? the accused tyrant? I see your point."

"Thank you," she said, "though wicked sarcasm never wins fair lady. Actually, I have a point, and it makes me mad. I'm thinking of going into paralegal work when I begin to lose my looks. Unless this writing deal goes down, in which case, I'll become an investigative reporter."

She pronounced "investigative" very well. She had a degree in speech from the University of California at Los Angeles. She didn't mean to quibble, her body's oratory sang, although her words quibbled a bit. The music of her face, that sulkiness and willfulness, that silken cajoling look, suddenly changed to fun: "I know how to do dirty things. Don't think I just learned them for work."

"Put that in."

"What?"

"In your story. Write it."

"Oh, man, I suppose you're right," and she laughed again, and it was as if the brooding never existed, and then she looked at me with desire—desire not for me but to be a writer—and asked: "It's hard, isn't it?"

"Yes. It's work. That's why it's fun, too."

She sighed. "Don't I know that story," she said.

The action here, I went away thinking, is going to be around the performance of literary criticism. And that was fine with me. For in this way I could be sure she was pure, I was clean, and our association would develop, as a man's and woman's must in these days, through a shared enterprise; in this case, the non-sexist one of helping her write the story of her servitude. I would avoid thinking too deeply about the implications.

She was curing herself through knowledge.

I was restoring a distracted soul to a new life as a new journalist.

But I said it was better not to think too much about the implications, didn't I? I went home and slept the sleep of the prospectively just. I took this rest on account.

She called a day later. She called *me*. My heart lifted. "I'm about ninety per cent there," she said.

"Fine. Let's meet when you've finished."

A few days later: "I'm ninety-nine per cent there."

"Ninety-nine?"

"Misspellings, punctuation, it's been so long since I was at UCLA."

"That's good enough. We meet. You bring xerox."

"Suppose I just drop it off and then you call me when you've read it?"

"Oh. Okay. Any time."

"And then you call me," she said. "We'll bring it up to a hundred . . . together . . ."

Who knows where the devil a fellow might find true love? Why not with a girl who practices the writing trade?

So it was with a thrill that I returned home from dinner with a friend in North Beach to find the envelope with my name on it plus her initials: L. A. Lydia Alsop. It sounded like a real name to go with her real feelings, not the pseudonym one gives an editor or a john. And so I took off jacket and shoes, poured a cup of ginseng tea for myself, and read:

> Who would ever guess that I, an upper class girl, raised in the heart of Westwood, California, with parents who loved me dearly and provided for my every need, would soon be laboring as a "hooker"—whore or prossie, though I prefer "White slave"—in a "Victorian-style" San Francisco sexual emporium? . . .

Oh dear. There were problems with the lead. The rhetorical question is a bit heavy, and the crowding of information, and the pinkie-pointed cuteness of the prose; and with the overuse of "quotation marks," could CAPITALIZATION be far behind? And hyperactive punctuation? No. For down a few more lines I found the short and dramatic paragraph:

> *Could I do this?* NO!!!

When she described her first "john" (her quotation marks) as "a tall, attractive blond," I knew there was also some feminism in here someplace. Women who refer to a man as "a blond" or "a dark, swarthy, but intelligent brunette" are usually making several points more than mere description of hair and skin color. I am capable of falling in love quickly, also out of love, and this was one of those cases. However, I am addicted to the language and to teaching. So I read on with red pencil in hand.

I noted that she should not describe people five times, as she did, as "attractive." An attractive junior college graduate . . . the attractive visiting nurse . . . an attractive Asian person . . . No. Dramatize, I commanded, make the reader see. Don't tell us what you think; give the reader the information which enables him to think and feel. Objective Correlative (I would explain about T. S. Eliot's critical point). Cognitive Dissonance (I would explain about the theory of brainwashing applied to literary art). Visualize. Make smells. Participate in the drama of the situation so that we are surprised by developments. Reveal your own character and that of your co-hookers; don't merely summarize. Put this work through the loom again.

In other words, the love system had been replaced in me by the pedagogical one. But who knows if perhaps they are not related?

The telephone rang and it was Lydia. "What per cent am I there?" she asked.

"Would you like to come over and we'll talk about it? I just finished reading."

"Aw gee thanks, that was really neat of you. What per cent?"

"Well, I think when you talked with me it was really interesting. Often people can tell a story better than they write it, they tense up, they think their words have to be . . . Well, I can't explain, but the flash in your eyes and how you smiled communicated something to me—"

"Wah? Wah you say?"

"I can explain if I show you my squiggles on your manuscript."

"You wrote on it in *pen?*"

"It's a xerox. Anyway, you need to do a lot of work—"

"I wanted to show it to a friend. Now he won't be able to read it—oh, shit. Okay, when can I pick it up?" She paused. "I mean I'm really grateful and I want to hear all you have to say, but I was hoping you would help me sell it to *Playboy* or *Esquire* or one of them, maybe *Ms*. But I'm coming over."

She was dressed for a conference, and again that heart-stopping loveliness. This is a metaphor; she didn't stop my heart; she raised my blood pressure with a little jolt. She was wearing pale horn-rimmed glasses that played enticingly against her glossy dark hair, her skin, her damp, soft, innocent mouth. I tried to recall how I had recently fallen out of love, due to prose. Now I was backsliding. "Rhetoric," I said. "Grammar. Syntax. Spelling. Coffee or ginseng tea?"

"You got anything to drink?"

"Scotch, vodka, gin."

"Whatever's right. Oh, scotch on rocks, you probably don't have any soda."

"That's the kind of insight we need in the piece," I said. "You're right, I don't carry the mixes."

As we settled down with the manuscript, I noticed a little lovely lithe dancer's twist of her waist. A delight. More delightful if it wasn't straining to look at my clock which was busily ticking away her valuable time. In my heart of hearts I began to wonder if she would listen to literary criticism if I offered to pay her fifty dollars to do so. "If you'd rather not talk about your piece, we could just talk," I said.

"No, no, I came here for that, I'm really . . ." That heart-breaking little smile. "I'm really interested, Herb. Critique away."

And so I delivered myself of a few general comments: frank, complete, open. Explore the whole creative writing approach. Understand that the reader knows nothing, may not even be interested, but you must interest him by engaging his attention. A kind of teasing, a kind of play. And good speech, Lydia, I explained, I mean good writing, tends to reflect good speech. "In real life you have a way of letting people know what you feel, and of getting their attention. You need to do this in your prose."

"Body English," she said. "My little moves. My forehand, my backhand. How I speak is with my little moves."

"Yes, yes, yes, but something of that is in good writing. It's almost a metabolic thing. Your writing style reflects your blood, your heart, your nervous system, how you digest and breathe—"

She began to look at me as if I were a freak who had freaky needs. She didn't like men who talk dirty (that was in the piece).

"Like when you describe your 'Patty Hearst Trip.' I mean, all in white, frills, a child's bed, dolls, and you tell them you're sixteen years old. That's a good incident. But I can imagine you doing that because I know you. The reader doesn't know you. You have to see the room, the furniture, what he says, what you say, what you do . . . I mean cuddle. I mean are you wearing perfume? I mean—well, it's your story."

She was thoughtful. She put down the drink. "You mean I have to make it more commercial?" she asked.

"That's a way of putting it. I mean you have to live through it more deeply."

"I was wearing Blue Grass cologne. Estelle gave it to me, it was her idea, I thought it was yucchy stuff."

"That's what we need to know. And tell about you and Estelle. You have to make it more dense, more vivid, you have to give us the details, exactly what happens."

Lydia smiled that heart-breaking corrupt smile at me, and having finished her glass and heard me out, rose with the graceful motion of a dancer; strong and practiced knees. A smile makes up for a lot. "I always know," she said, "an old guy like you—you're not so old, but I mean in his heart—I mean it takes someone who's been through what I have to appreciate my writing."

My reading skills were on the line. I loved her a lot less now. I no longer saw the incipient jowl, but I saw an argument. "You mean a limited audience of ex-hookers?" I asked. "I don't know if there's an alumni journal, my dear."

"You're trying to be funny, I can see that. You're trying to be sarcastic. Well, it only shows one thing." She picked up her manuscript. She held it by the neck. "You try, it proves," she said, "you try to break into a new field and the folks who are already there, they have the ins, they know the editors, they won't let you. But I'm not going to talk dirty for anyone."

INDEX

Alchemy: 11, 19, 24, 25 n.1
Alger, Horatio: 9
Alice in Wonderland (Carroll): 90
Allegory: 19, 28 n.31, 41, 78, 81
All in the Wrong (wrongly cited): 12
America: 5, 7, 9, 79, 83, 94, 96, 116, 117, 119; culture in, 5; authors in, 5, 7, 10; and the novel, 5; public in, 8; Jews in, 10; and paper money, 15, 18; cipher writing in, 22
American Association for the Advancement of Science: 19
American Renaissance (Matthiessen): 5
Aristotle: 20, 24–25, 37, 73, 74, 75, 91
Art and Revolution (Wagner): 100
Auden, W. H.: 53
Austen, Jane: 72
Avant Garde: 4, 7

Baker, Carlos: 52
Baker, Sheridan: 57
Baltimore, Maryland: 7
Balzac, Honoré de: 4, 75
Banker's Daughter, The (Morris): 13
Baudelaire, Charles: 7, 12, 119
Bellow, Saul: 4, 9–10, 111–21, 124
Best sellers: 4, 6, 7, 8
"Big Two-Hearted River" (Hemingway): 60
Blake, William: 77, 91
"Blue Hotel, The" (Crane): 83–84
Boni and Liveright (publishers): 53
Book of Daniel, The (Doctorow): 79, 81, 88–91
Bosch, Hieronymus: 76
Boswell, James: 130
Boys of Summer, The (Kahn): 130
Brecht, Bertolt: 79
Brooks, Cleanth: 4

Brown, Charles Brockden: 6
Brown, Norman O.: 73ff.
Bruce, Lenny: 10
Burlesque: 19

Cannell, Kitty (Hemingway's friend): 52
Cantos (Pound): 95
Capitalism: 8, 27 n.18, 74ff., 99, 100; *see also* money
Carnegie, Andrew: 9
Catch-22 (Heller): 4, 111
Cather, Willa: 130
Charlotte Temple (Rowson): 6
Christ: 73, 74, 91
Ciphers: 11, 22, 23, 24
"Clean, Well-Lighted Place, A" (Hemingway): 51
Clemens, Samuel: *see* Twain, Mark
Cleveland, Ohio: 106
Cobbett, William: 15
Cognitive dissonance: 140
Comley, Nancy: 51
Commerce: 93ff.; and art, 5, 93, 105, 106, 107; *see also* money
Contracts: 2–3, 31
Coover, Robert: 94
Cowley, Malcolm: 52
Crane, Hart: 106
Crane, Stephen: 83–84

"D" (reviewer of "The Gold-Bug"): 12ff.
Dante: 61
Democratic Review: 19
Derrida, Jacques: 75
Devil, the: 24, 30 n.52, 78, 87, 100
Dialect: 23–24
"Diamond as Big as the Ritz, A" (Fitzgerald): 8
Dickens, Charles: 4, 34, 35

145

Diderot, Denis: 74
Dionysius: 7
Disneyland: 90
Doctorow, E. L.: 71–92
Dollar Newspaper: 13, 14
Donaldson, Scott: 53
Dreiser, Theodore: 111
Dylan, Bob: 86

Eliot, George (Mary Ann Evans): 72
Eliot, T. S.: 140
Emerson, Ralph Waldo: 22–23
Empedocles: 95, 100 ff.
Enlightenment: 86
Entomology: 12, 14, 24, 25
Ernest Hemingway: A Life Story (Baker): 52
Esquire: 3, 127, 141
Euripides: 7
Europe (medieval): 74
Evans, Mary Ann: *see* George Eliot
Executioner's Song, The (Mailer): 94

Faulkner, William: 4
Fitzgerald, F. Scott: 4, 7, 8, 10, 57, 116
Ford, Henry: 81
Fords, the: 4
Foster, Stephen: 123
France: and Poe, 6; and American culture, 7
Freud, Sigmund: 13, 25 n.11, 73, 75, 76, 91; Reality Principle, 5
Fuller, Buckminster: 89
"Future of the Novel, The" (James): 47

Gaddis, William: 93–109
Germany: 19, 52, 100
Gibbs, Josiah Willard: 104
Gilded Age, the: 8
Gilmore, Gary: 94
God: 19, 24, 75, 77
" 'Gold-Bug'—a Decided Humbug, The" ("D"): 13–14
"Gold-Bug, The" (Poe): 8, 9, 11–30
Goldman, Emma: 80, 82
Goldwyn, Samuel: 5
Gone with the Wind (Mitchell): 6

"Gonzaga Manuscripts, The" (Bellow): 112
Graham's: 13
Gravity's Rainbow: (Pynchon): 93, 94
Griswold, Rufus: 7, 8, 9
Guggenheims, the: 4
Guthrie, Pat (Hemingway's friend): 52

Harcourt (publisher): 53
Hawkes, John: 111
Hawthorne, Nathaniel: 6, 20
Heller, Joseph: 4, 111
Hemingway, Ernest: 4, 51–69
Hemingway, Hadley (Hemingway's first wife): 53
"Hemingway, Money, and *The Sun Also Rises*" (Sugg): 51
Heraclitus: 25
Hitler, Adolf: 138
Hogarth, William: 115
Holland, Laurence: 41
Hollywood: 4, 7
Homer: 95
Homer, Winslow: 80
Homonymity: 21
Huckleberry Finn (Twain): 6, 9, 90
Humboldt's Gift (Bellow): 9–10, 94, 111–21

"It's Alright Ma, I'm Only Bleeding" (Dylan): 86

Jackson, Andrew: 19
James, Henry: 31–49, 128
Jameson, Fredric: 71, 75
James, William: 45
Johnson, Samuel: 5, 93
Journals: commercial, 3, 8; subsidized, 3
Joyce, James: 95
JR (Gaddis): 93–109

Kafka, Franz: 78
Kahn, Roger: 130
Keats, John: 36
Kennedy, John Pendleton: 19
"King Pest" (Poe): 19
Knopf (publisher): 53

INDEX

Language: 18, 22–23, 85–86, 94, 100, 101, 103, 107; *see also* dialect
Lasch, Christopher: 76
"Last Judgement, The" (Bosch): 76
Lawrence, D. H.: 5
"Lesson of Balzac, The" (James): 39
Lewis, Robert W.: 57
Liberal Imagination, The (Trilling): 75
Life Against Death (Brown): 76
Literary World: 13
Literature: women in, 6, 8; *see also* money
Locke, Richard Adams: 19
Loeb, Harold (Hemingway's friend): 52
"Looking for Mr. Green" (Bellow): 111
Luce, Henry: 4
Lucre: *see* money
Luther, Martin: 76, 78

McLuhan, Marshall: 89
Mailer, Norman: 4, 9, 94
Mallarmé, Stéphane: 7
Marxism: 4, 71, 73, 123, 126, 130
Marx, Karl: 23, 29 n.43, 71 ff.
Mass audience: 5, 8
Mass production: 5
Masters, Edgar Lee: 123
Matthiessen, F. O.: 5
Melville, Herman: 5ff., 14, 93
Merchant of Venice, The (Shakespeare): 95
Metaphor: 41, 52, 53, 89, 112
Metonymy: 20
MGM (studios): 4
Miller, Arthur: 4
Milton, John: 35
Mitchell, Margaret: 6
Moby Dick (Melville): 6, 8, 93
Modernism: 4, 5
Money: and the arts, 1, 31, 35, 36, 54, 94, 100, 105, 117, 131; and literature, 1–10, 31, 71–73, 111, 113, 116, 123, 127, 128, 132, 134; as symbol, 11, 14, 15, 18–23, 24, 35; and excrement, 13, 73, 76, 77, 78, 82–83, 87–88, 98, 100; and imagination, 13; and language, 18, 22–23, 94, 107; and writing, 18; and religion, 54, 55, 77, 81, 98; *see also* capitalism, commerce, *and* usury

Morgan, J. P.: 81, 82
Morris, Robert: 13
Mother Courage and Her Children (Brecht): 79
Mr. Sammler's Planet (Bellow): 112
Ms.: 141
My Fair Lady (musical): 5

National Book Award: 93
Naturalism: 77, 111
Nesbit, Evelyn: 80
New Era: 19
New Testament: 74
New York City: 79
New York Times Book Review, The: 3
Nietzsche, Friedrich: 73, 75, 78
Nobel Prize: 9, 10
Norris, Frank: 94

Objective correlative: 140
O'Connor, Flannery: 111, 132
Octopus, The (Norris): 94
Odyssey (Homer): 95
Onomatopoeia: 21
On the Equilibrium of Heterogeneous Substances (Gibbs): 104
"Oration Delivered at the Democratic Republican Celebration of the 64th Anniversary of the United States" (Young): 15
O'Sullivan, John L.: 19
Our Mutual Friend (Dickens): 33, 34

Pamplona, Spain: 52
Paper Against Gold (Cobbett): 15
Paradigms: 43, 44, 46
Paradise Lost (Milton): 35, 93, 100
"Paradox of Political Economy" (Clinton): 19
Paris, France: 52
"Paul's Case" (Cather): 130
Persephone (Zuntz): 101
Pfeiffer, Pauline (Hemingway's second wife): 53
Pierre (Melville): 8
Pittsburgh Steelers: 124, 128
Plato: 37
Playboy: 3, 141

PMLA: 3
Poe, Edgar Allan: 6ff., 11–30
Politics (Aristotle): 74
Portrait of a Lady, The (James): 31–49
Pound, Ezra: 95
"Power of Money in Bourgeois Society, The" (Marx): 74
Princeton University Press: 4
Public Burning, The (Coover): 94
Puns: 21, 23, 24, 25, 53
Pygmalion (Shaw): 5
Pynchon, Thomas: 9, 94, 111

Quodlibet (Kennedy): 19

Rabelais, François: 87
Ragtime (Doctorow): 79–83, 84
Rameau's Nephew (Diderot): 74–75
Ray, Aldo: 86
Realism: 40, 72, 78, 83, 111
Recognitions, The (Gaddis): 93
Restoration drama: 72
Richardson, Samuel: 4
Ring des Nibelungen, Der (Wagner): 95ff., 108
Robbins, Harold: 4, 9
Rockefellers, the: 4
Rogers, Henry (Vice President of Standard Oil): 9
Roosevelt, Clinton: 19
Rosenberg, Ethel: 89
Rosenberg, Julius: 89
Rosenfeld, Isaac (Bellow's friend): 10
Rovit, Earl: 51
Rowson, Susanna: 6

Salinger, J. D.: 9
Sartre, Jean-Paul: 87
Satire: 19, 60
Scarlet Letter, The (Hawthorne): 6
Schulberg, Budd: 8, 9
Schwartz, Delmore: 10
Scott, Walter: 35
Scribner, Charles (publisher): 53
Segal, Erich: 4
Seize the Day (Bellow): 112
"Seven Vagabonds, The" (Hawthorne): 20

Shakespeare, William: 4
Shaw, George Bernard: 5
Simmel, Georg: 34
Simon and Schuster (publishers): 4
Snow White: 90
"Soldier's Home" (Hemingway): 60
Sot-Weed Factor, The (Barth): 93
South Carolina: 23
Spender, Stephen: 1
"Sphinx, The" (Poe): 13
Sprague, Claire: 51
Steiner, George: 107
Stevenson, Robert Louis: 35
Stewart, Don (Hemingway's friend): 52
Stowe, Harriet Beecher: 6, 8
Studies in Classic American Literature (Lawrence): 5
Sugg, Richard: 51
Sullivan Island (setting for "The Gold-Bug"): 12
Sun Also Rises, The (Hemingway): 51–69
Susann, Jacqueline: 4, 6, 9
Symbol: 11, 13, 14, 15, 18–23, 24, 25, 115
Synecdoche: 43
Synopsis of Natural History (Wyatt): 12

Tennyson, Alfred: 77
Ten Thousand a Year (Warren): 11
Thoreau, Henry David: 125ff.
Times Literary Supplement, The: 3
Tom Sawyer (Twain): 9
Tortesa the Usurer (Willis): 24
Tragedy: 59, 60
Trilling, Lionel: 75
Twain, Mark (Samuel Clemens): 4, 8–9
Twysden, Lady Duff (Hemingway's friend): 52
Typee (Melville): 8

Ulysses (Joyce): 93, 95
Uncle Tom's Cabin (Stowe): 6
Understanding Fiction (Brooks and Warren): 4
United States: *see* America
Universal Films: 130

INDEX

Use and Abuse of History, The (Nietzsche): 79
Usury: 24, 76, 93–109; Aristotle on, 20, 24–25, 74

Vachel Lindsay (Masters): 123
Van Buren, Martin: 19
Vanity Presses: 2
Vogue: 53

Wagner, Richard: 95ff.
Waiting for Cordelia (Gold): 137
Wall Street Journal, The: 97
Warren, Robert Penn: 4
Warren, Samuel: 11

Welcome to Hard Times (Doctorow): 79, 82, 83–88
Westerns: 79, 83ff.
Whitman, Walt: 1, 130
Wiener, Norbert: 104
Wilde, Oscar: 108
Williams, Raymond: 72
Wise Blood (O'Connor): 111
Wittgenstein, Ludwig: 23
Wordsworth, William: 91
Wylder, Delbert E.: 54

Young, Samuel: 15

Zola, Émile: 77
Zuntz, Gunther: 101